I AM FIRST A HUMAN BEING

DI023285

940.5472
W788

I Am First a Human Being

THE PRISON LETTERS OF KRYSTYNA WITUSKA

EDITED AND TRANSLATED

BY IRENE TOMASZEWSKI

LIBRARY ST. MARY'S COLLEGE

Véhicule Press

Cover designed by J.W. Stewart
Cover photo and family photos courtesy of Tomasz Steppa
Letter on page 28 courtesy of
University of Warsaw Library, Manuscript Archives
All other photos courtesy of Archives of the Main Commission
for the Investigation of Crimes Against the Polish Nation, Warsaw
Typeset in Perpetua by Simon Garamond
Printed by AGMV Marquis

Translation and Introduction Copyright © Irene Tomaszewski 1997
Dépôt légal, Bibliothèque nationale du Québec
and the National Library of Canada, fourth quarter 1997

All rights reserved.

CANADIAN CATALOGUING IN PUBLICATION DATA
Wituska, Krystyna
I am first a human being : the prison letters
of Krystyna Wituska

ISBN 1-55065-095-5

1. Wituska, Krystyna–Correspondence.
2. World War, 1939-1945–Underground movements–
Poland–Biography. 3. World War, 1939-1945–Prisoners
and prisons, German–Biography.
4. Women–spies–Poland–Biography.
I. Tomaszewski, Irene. II. Title

D805.G3W576 1997   940.53'37'092   C97-900983-9

Published by Véhicule Press,
P.O.B. 125, Place du Parc Station,
Montreal, Quebec, Canada H2W 2M9

http://www.cam.org/~vpress

Printed in Canada on alkaline paper.

Acknowledgements

The translation of the letters in *I Am First a Human Being* is based in large part on the Polish edition of the letters of Krystyna Wituska, *Na Granicy Zycia i Smierci: Listy i grypsy wiezienne Krystyny Wituskiej*, [On the Frontier of Life and Death: Official and Smuggled Prison Letters of Krystyna Wituska] published by Panstwowy Instytut Wydawniczy (Warsaw 1970), edited and with an introduction by the historian Wanda Kiedrzynska. The publisher, PIW, is no longer in existence and Dr. Kiedrzynska is no longer living. During my research in Poland in February and March 1997 I tried to locate members of Dr. Kiedrzynska's family or someone connected with this publication, without success. I wish to acknowledge my indebtedness to the work of Dr. Kiedrzynska.

I would like to thank Dr. Irena Bellert of Rawdon, Quebec, for bringing Krystyna's letters to my attention, for her reading of my translation and introduction, for her corrections and suggestions, and for putting me in touch with Tomasz Steppa, Krystyna's nephew, in Warsaw. Dr. Bellert, a cousin of Krystyna's, also wrote to Maria Kacprzyk-Tabeau, who had shared a prison cell with Krystyna Wituska in Berlin, and who was kind enough to read the text and send further information and clarification.

It was particularly moving to meet Tomasz Steppa—the little "Kola" in Krystyna's letters—who gave me photos from his family albums and a copy of his mother's unpublished memoirs. These, together with his recollections of family history, provided me with a picture of life on his grandparents' estate before the war. For this, and also for the warm hospitality of both Tomasz and his wife Basia, I am very grateful.

Many thanks to Mrs. Izabela Borowicz and her colleagues at the Main Commission for the Investigation of Crimes Against the Polish Nation for their help and friendship while I was in Warsaw. I am also indebted to the staff at the University of Warsaw Library (Manuscript Archives) and to Stefan Wladysiuk at the Polish Library of McGill University in Montreal.

My dear friend, Malgorzata Dzieduszycka, can never be thanked enough for her enthusiasm and encouragement when she was Consul-General in Montreal, and whose hospitality in Warsaw was without bounds. Thanks also to Brian McKenna and to Arnie Gelbart of Gala Films for providing access to an unpublished interview with Helga Grimpe; to Michal Bukojemski of Warsaw for his help with photos; to Brian McCordick and Joan McCordick for translating the German prayer which appears in one of the letters; Alex di Meo for his usual patient reading; and Wanda Muszynska and Joanna Kranz for their friendship.

Finally, I wish to express my gratitude to the Polish Socio-cultural Foundation of Quebec for their generous support.

Contents

Preface

DURING THE PAST FIVE YEARS I have interviewed more than a hundred people who survived the German occupation of Poland. With a startling frequency during the interviews they would begin a sentence with: "The day before the war....." then go on to say it was his mother's birthday; that she went shopping with her mother to buy new clothes for school; or that he was riding on a tram when a lovely young girl got on and he remembered exactly what she was wearing and the cut of her hair—the day before the war began.

From one day to the next, everything we know—and they knew—as human rights was gone, including the right to life itself. "The day before the war" marked the last day of all that was normal and the beginning of a life of terror and brutality; a horror for which no one was prepared.

The letters of Krystyna Wituska constitute a personal memoir of one such young life, documenting both a carefree, normal life before the war and the cruelty that came with the Occupation. The letters constitute a narrative, a story of the love and friendship which sustain the human spirit through great adversity and of a defiance and determination that allowed Krystyna and her friends to face life and death on their terms and not on those of their tormentors.

I translated some of Krystyna Wituska's letters for a

documentary on Poland made by Brian McKenna for the Canadian Broadcasting Corporation's documentary series, "Witness." The response, first from people involved in the production and then from the public, encouraged me to translate the entire collection.

The English translation of Krystyna Wituska's letters and much of the historical background for this book are based on Wanda Kiedrzynska's book, *Na Granicy Zycia i Smierci:Listy i Grypsy Wiezenne Krystyny Wituskiej* (On the Frontier of Life and Death: Official and Smuggled Prison Letters of Krystyna Wituska), published in Poland in 1970. The original letters to her parents are housed in the Manuscript Archives of the University of Warsaw Library, while the smuggled letters to Helga Grimpe were turned over to the Archives of the Main Commission for the Investigation of Crimes Against the Polish Nation after the war. The book also includes some letters that were the property of Dr. Kiedrzynska. Further information about the prisoners was obtained from *Slownik uczestniczek walki o niepodleglosc Polski 1939-1945: Polegle i zmarle w okresie okupacji niemieckiej* (A Dictionary of the Dead and Missing Women of the Underground During the German Occupation 1939-1945), published by the Panstwowy Instytut Wydawniczy, Warsaw, 1988.

Biographical data about the family and photographs were obtained from Krystyna Wituska's nephew, Tomasz Steppa, and from an unpublished memoir written by his mother (Krystyna's sister). Maria Kacprzyk-Tabeau, a former cell-mate of Krystyna's in the Alt-Moabit Prison and now a resident of Gdansk, also provided some new information. Finally, a 1994 interview with Helga Grimpe in Germany provided further insights into the relationship between Krystyna and the compassionate and courageous Grimpes—mother and daughter. When available, I have added information about the relationship to Krystyna of the people she writes about, and about their ultimate fate.

All of the letters to Helga Grimpe, the teen-aged daughter of the prison guard Hedwig Grimpe, affectionately known as *Sonnenschein*—Sunshine, and the letters to Gerd and Ursel Terwiel, the brother and sister of the German dissident and fellow prisoner, Mimi Turwiel, were smuggled out of the prison by Mrs. Grimpe, as were a few of the letters to Krystyna's parents. The letters to Helga Grimpe and the Turwiels were originally written in German, as were some of the letters to Krystyna's parents when permission to write in Polish was denied. These have been translated from Wanda Kiedrzynska's Polish rendition.

I tried as much as possible to maintain the emotional nuances of Krystyna Wituska's letters—English is a difficult language in which to express the many degrees of intimacy and affection that the Polish permits. To avoid confusing the English reader I mostly kept to one form of a name, although in the Polish a variety of diminutives was used. For example, within the family, Krystyna's sister Halina would be addressed as Halinka. The diminutive indicates a close relationship, or sheds light on the mood of the writer. These are not available to us in English, and adding the adjective "little" every time would be both tiresome and imprecise. It should also be noted that the masculine and feminine forms of Polish family names are slightly different. So while Krystyna's surname is Watuska, her father's is Wituski and we refer to her home as the Wituski family estate.

These and some other interpretative liberties, notably in punctuation and use of idioms, have not, I hope, altered Krystyna's own literary "voice," certainly one of the most distinctive voices I have encountered in any literature. Facing death, she concentrated on life—her own intellectual and spiritual development, her family, her friends, all the unknown victims who shared her fate, as well as her vision of the world as it should be and the choices she and so many others made, at great cost, to defend that vision.

In the introduction, I have provided a brief background to her letters based on the sources cited above. While I hope this background is helpful, I believe that the letters of Krystyna Wituska constitute a rare example of a personal testament that needs little introduction.

Introduction

KRYSTYNA WITUSKA, who joined the Polish Underground when she was twenty-one years old, wrote in one of her letters from prison, "I am first a human being, and only then a Pole." She wrote these words to emphasize that her ordeal did not turn her into a nationalist, that her first identity was that of a human being. It is her humanity that unites her not only with other victims of war and other resistance fighters, but also enables us all to identify with her even though her ordeal was outside the scope of our experience.

Krystyna wrote these letters in the last year of her life, in a Gestapo prison in Berlin. She was condemned to death by guillotine, but she wrote about life. She missed the sound of music, revelled in the beauty of a blue sky and treetops glimpsed through her prison window, and tap danced in her cell to exercise and to keep warm. During a brief outing, she lifted her face to the sun for the sensual pleasure—and declared it "better than a kiss." While in solitary confinement, she acknowledged the spider in the corner of her cell as her only companion. Outside of solitary, she formed intense friendships, a community of prisoners.

Krystyna was born on May 12, 1920, the younger daughter of Feliks Wituski and Maria Orzechowska, and grew up on their country estate, Jerzew, in Wartheland, an area of western Poland. Her father, to whom Krystyna was very close, was an agronomist and her letters reveal Krystyna's interest in his work as well as her own love of nature—of the meadows, wild flowers and birds of the countryside.

Krystyna and her sister Halina were educated at home, first with a governess who was instructed to speak to them only in French, and then others who prepared them for admission to high school, a convent in the city of Poznan. As privileged children of the landed gentry, the two girls enjoyed a life of parties with other young people, but even more, they enjoyed the freedom of country life—running barefoot all summer, swimming, tree-climbing, overnight bicycle tours, and best of all, accompanying their father on his rounds of the estate. In their own "zoological garden," they kept a variety of birds, insects, snakes and animals, which they often used mischievously in merciless pranks on their unsuspecting urban, governesses.

After high school, Halina went on to further study in horticulture but Krystyna, suffering from respiratory illness, possibly incipient tuberculosis, was sent to a private school in Switzerland in the hope that the fresh mountain air would be therapeutic. As war clouds rumbled over Europe in 1939, Krystyna begged her parents to allow her to come home to be with her family. Invasion had long been a tragic part of Polish history, but nobody, at this point, expected a war of such unparalleled savagery.

Just before going off to Switzerland, Krystyna got engaged to Zbyszek Walc, a childhood friend and a son of another prominent family, Drs. Wanda and Lucian Walc, who owned a well known private medical clinic in Warsaw. The young people were fond of one another but it was not a mature love, at least not on Krystyna's part, and she didn't give it much thought as she departed for her school in Neuchâtel.

When she returned in the summer of 1939, Zbyszek, an officer cadet, had already been mobilized and her father, a reserve officer, was called to service in Warsaw. During the month long

Krystyna (clutching her father's leg), and her sister Halina
"enjoyed the freedom of country life—running barefoot"
on the Wituski country estate.

battle that ended with Poland's defeat, Zbyszek was taken prisoner. Her father returned home after the capitulation of Warsaw.

Soon after the conquest, Poland was partitioned by Germany and her then ally, the Soviet Union. The Wituski's estate was in Western Poland, the area immediately incorporated into the German Reich.

The Occupation was established with extreme terror from the beginning. In the annexed territories, Poles and Jews were ruthlessly evicted from their homes which were turned over to German colonists. Thousands were summarily shot, some two million were transported in cattle cars to the central part of Poland, an area renamed simply the *Generalgouvernement*[1]; thousands more were arrested and sent to concentration camps in Germany, while the rest were kept for forced labour.

For a short time, the Wituski's estate, isolated from major roads, was left in peace and the family took in a young man, Janusz Steppa, who had been expelled from his home near Gdansk (Danzig). Steppa began tutoring the young women in German, providing some continuity in their interrupted education. In December, 1939, German patrols arrived, giving the family fifteen minutes to pack one suitcase each, and deported them to the *Generalgouvernement*.

For a few weeks the family found shelter wherever they could, in barns, stables and finally on a small farm abandoned by ethnic Germans who moved to the incorporated territories where they took over a confiscated Polish estate. It was there, that the two sisters discovered that their parents' marriage had been an unhappy one, kept together by agreement until their daughters married.

Without a home to sustain them, the family split up. Krystyna and her mother went to Warsaw to live with relatives;

Mr. Wituski, and the woman he had loved for many years, found work on an estate that had been taken over by German authorities. Halina married the tutor, Janusz Steppa, and the young couple set out together to find a refuge for themselves. Although Krystyna wrote lovingly to all of them in one shared letter, she frequently expressed her anxiety about her mother, alone with her grief, and repeatedly asked her father and sister to take special care of her.

In Warsaw, Krystyna ran into Karol Szapiro, a young man she met early in the war when both families found temporary shelter in a church. Karol, a Jewish student who had escaped with his family from Lodz, was living under an assumed identity with forged documents. Krystyna and Karol fell in love, a mature, passionate love. It was imperative to protect his identity, and even in prison, she never wrote to him directly but in her guarded messages to him, and enquiries about him, she often referred to him as her old tutor.

For a while, Krystyna shared a room with a very young aunt, Alina, whose husband had been killed in the first months of the war. Alina ran a shop designated for Poles with ration coupons and arranged a job for Krystyna in the stockroom. The two women became close friends. Eventually Krystyna moved in with her mother who had rented a room in the home of some Warsaw friends. It was there that Krystyna was arrested.

Krystyna's experiences—being evicted from their home, transported like cattle, and left to eke out a living—convinced her that Poles must resist and maintain their dignity, whatever the cost, in the face of the enemy's policy of humiliation. She probably got involved in the underground quite early, though the need for secrecy precluded any discussions of her activities. It is known, however, that by late 1941, she was involved with the ZWZ (Union for Armed Resistance), a precursor of the *Armia*

Krajowa (Home Army), the military side of the underground state responsible to the Government-in-Exile in London. By her own admission, she was at first attracted by the excitement of resistance and didn't consider the danger, but youthful bravado soon turned into a mental and spiritual mastery over fear.

Krystyna was assigned to an espionage cell in Warsaw, first to get information about military movements at the airport, and then to gather information about the location of certain squadrons of the *Wehrmacht*—the German army—the strength of the battalions and the names of officers. At one point, a German officer told her he knew what she was doing but that he would say nothing if she stopped immediately. She stopped, but only temporarily.

In June 1942, anticipating arrest, she left Warsaw and spent some time with a cousin in the country. When she returned, she was assigned to a new cell at which time she met Maria [Marysia] Kacprzyk, a chemistry student, and another young woman, Wanda Kaminska. A short time later she was arrested. Searching her room, the Gestapo found the addresses of her two colleagues, who were arrested the following night.

Krystyna was taken to Pawiak, the main prison in Warsaw, and was interrogated at Aleja Szucha, the notorious interrogation centre of the Gestapo headquarters. It is not known how severe her interrogations were.

In one of her letters, Krystyna writes about being taken in a Gestapo van from the prison to Aleja Szucha. She describes her feelings as she watched people on the street, seemingly carefree and indifferent to the plight of the prisoners. This feeling of isolation is common among prisoners in repressive regimes; they feel cut off from the outside world and think they have been forgotten. Krystyna had no doubt seen arrests, prison vans, and perhaps even public executions; she knew that the people were helpless and in constant danger, and that they could not help her. This was the only time she expressed this such feeling of abandonment. More often, she writes movingly about the pain of those who can do nothing to help their loved ones but can only wait and worry about their children, their parents, their friends.

On October 22, 1942, Krystyna was transported to the military prison on Alexanderplatz in Berlin. With her were three other Polish women including Cezara Dickstein, an older woman who was Krystyna's "prison mother" those first few weeks, and Olga Jedrkiewicz, the cheerful "Olenka" who would later share cell #18 with Krystyna after their transfer to the interrogation prison, Alt-Moabit.

Ironically, Krystyna and Zbyszek, who had not seen one another since she left for school in Switzerland in the fall of 1938, were to meet again in Berlin, at the Alexanderplatz and Alt-Moabit prisons, where both were brought for interrogation. Zbyszek, who had been captured on October 25, 1939 as a prisoner-of-war, had first been taken to Itzehoe camp and then to Stalag II Neubrandenburg. In March, 1942, he was released from the POW camp but kept in Germany for forced labour. This was counter to the POW policy of the Geneva convention but a common practice in Nazi Germany. Prisoners were 'released' into the hands of the Gestapo which profited by supplying forced labour to the Reich.

In Germany, Zbyszek linked up with a Polish underground network that sent reports to Poland about the conditions of Polish prisoners there. One of his reports was intercepted, and in a search of his belongings, the Gestapo found Krystyna's address. It was this, rather than her own work in the underground, that brought her to the attention of the Gestapo and led to her arrest. Krystyna and Zbyszek, along with all their other friends in the

Berlin prison, were brought to trial—though these trials were nothing more than a facade for domestic consumption in Germany to maintain the impression that the Nazis continued to respect the old justice system. Krystyna was called to testify at Zbyszek's trial and was still at Alt-Moabit Prison when she learned that he was spared the death penalty and was sentenced to serve a term in prison. But in reality, whatever the sentence, few prisoners ever made it home again. Once they had served their terms, they were released to the Gestapo who transported them to concentration camps. When Zbyszek finished his prison term he was sent first to the Sachsenhausen concentration camp and then to Buchenwald. When Buchenwald was evacuated in April 1945, friends who escaped from the forced march testified later that he was burnt to death, along with the other prisoners, in a barn in Gardelegen. Before her death Krystyna learned that Zbyszek had 'disappeared,' that is, his family no longer had any contact with him but she held out hope that he was still alive somewhere in the Nazi penal system. In the end, both Krystyna and Zbyszek died not knowing the other's fate.

It was while Krystyna was at Alt-Moabit, in the summer of 1943, that she got word that her beloved Karol had disappeared. Before that, Krystyna had been sending messages to Karol in her letters to her mother; writing to him directly might have endangered him. Her letters reveal great anxiety about his fate. Karol Szapiro was arrested in 1943 at the railway station in Siedlce and was shot, possibly because his Jewish identity was revealed. Her family spared her this tragic news. In one of her last letters she asked, "Where can he be?"

In her letters Krystyna was quite candid that she did not love her fiancé, Zbyszek, though she saw no reason to break their engagement since she was going to die anyway. She didn't want to hurt him needlessly, and she also believed that he needed all his emotional strength to survive his own ordeal with the Gestapo. According to friend and fellow prisoner Maria Kacprzyk, Karol was and remained Krystyna's real love.

It was at the 'Alex,' as she later called Alexanderplatz, that Krystyna met Mimi Terwiel, with whom she shared a cell for several weeks. Maria Terwiel (Mimi), ten years older than Krystyna, was a German dissident, a lawyer who, together with her fiancé Hans Helmut Himpel, was a member of an anti-Nazi conspiracy, *Die Schulze-Boysen / Harnack Organization-Rote Kapelle*. This was a Soviet-backed organization set up in all German-occupied countries for the purposes of espionage; in Germany it attracted opponents of the regime who had few other places to turn to for organized resistance. The Gestapo cracked the *Rote-Kapelle* in 1942, arrested its members and destroyed most of its records. From a Gestapo document dated December 29, 1942, we know that half of its membership comprised women and young girls. Mimi and Hans were Social Democrats, not Communists, but the *Rote-Kapelle* provided them with the means for resistance. According to Maria Kacprzyk, it is doubtful that Mimi realized the full extent of the organization's activities.

Whether Mimi Terwiel influenced Krystyna, or whether they were simply a personality match is hard to say. Krystyna does say that it was from Mimi that she learned to act defiant, to never show any fear, and to treat her captors with contempt. But this was very much the way Krystyna was described by her friends as well, and in many of her letters about Mimi, it is the younger woman who seems to have comforted the older one. The two women discussed the death penalty—and the option of suicide. "Mimi said she would not wait patiently like a sheep until they killed her," wrote Krystyna, but in the end, they decided that they must leave to the Nazis the moral responsibility for their deaths.

Each helped the other face death with courage and with prayer. Krystyna asked her mother to remember Mimi in her prayers, and Mimi, before her death, wrote out an ancient German prayer for Krystyna. Krystyna did not pray with an immature hope for special favours; she prayed only for spiritual strength, for the courage to accept death on her terms, so that she would not, at the end, be reduced to an "animal-like struggle to live" at all costs. She struggled with her faith, at times finding solace and strength, at other times questioning the point of everything. In a letter to Zbyszek's mother, she admitted that she had become less religious, a situation she described as both awful and odd, "...but I can't be religious just because there is no other way out." It would be "presumptuous," she continued, to ask God to save her life. "Why should I have a greater right to life than those millions who have already perished in this terrible war?"

In February 1943 Krystyna was transferred to the Alt-Moabit prison, where some of the conditions, such as food and hygiene, were a bit better, but overall, it was harsher, and for the first few months Krystyna was in solitary confinement. She was given a sewing machine and worked all day, stopping only for one meal. It was boring work and she missed companionship. "You can cry by yourself," she wrote, "but to laugh, you need a friend. I tried it once but couldn't continue. One soon feels one is going insane."

After the trials, and pending ratification of the sentences— death in most cases—prisoners were taken out of solitary, though they were still obliged to work, sewing dresses, blouses and purses for German civilians. Krystyna, now in a cell with Monika Dymska and Olenka Jedrkiewicz, all condemned to death, felt that condemned prisoners should be spared this indignity. She would much rather read, she wrote. In fact, prison made her realize that more than anything else, she would like to study and decided that if by some miracle she were to survive, that would be her first objective.

Their sentences came as no surprise. At the end of 1942, after the German defeat at Stalingrad, Hitler ordered a mandatory death sentence for all spies and communists, and only those prisoners held on lesser charges got terms in penal or concentration camps. Still, the *drei Polen Kinder* [three Polish children], as Mimi Terwiel called the trio in cell #18, appealed their sentences, hoping to be included in an amnesty proclaimed by Hitler to mark the tenth anniversary of the Nazis' election to power.

Cell #18 was "the most cheerful cell at Moabit." Waiting to hear the outcome of their appeal, Krystyna, Monika and Olenka sang all their old songs, told jokes, and discussed life. A woman must have a profession, Krystyna wrote, but she also should have a family. A woman confined to the home is as incomplete as is the woman who knows nothing of family life. It would be hard, after their experiences, to find a man who would measure up to their standards, she decided; they had learned so much, had grown so strong. They couldn't settle for just anyone. She also noted—with apologies if it sounded conceited—that women, in general, handle death much more bravely than men do.

While Krystyna waited for the decision on her appeal, one by one, her friends' lives were settled. Some were transferred to various camps, while others were taken to Plotzensee, the prison where they were guillotined. Each chance at life was wildly celebrated; each death bitterly mourned.

In March 1943, two fellow prisoners, Wieslawa Jezierska and Olga Kaminska, were executed. They had both worked with a Polish-Yugoslav unit helping British POWs escape from

Kazamat Fortu VII, an old, windowless, fortress-like Prussian prison, in Poznan and escorted them south and across the Bulgarian-Turkish border. Olga had met and married a young Pole who was trying to get to Palestine to join the Polish forces there. He was caught when the Germans entered Yugoslavia. Olga and Wieslawa were caught on the Serb-Bulgarian border in the company of two British officers, identified only by their surnames, Sinclair and Littledale. Pregnant, Olga was kept in a Belgrade prison until she gave birth, after which her son, Marek was sent to a *Kinderheim*—an orphanage—and she to Alt-Moabit. Because of her son, she had asked for clemency but was denied. She managed to get word to her parents about the boy and they eventually recovered him.

Olenka's death sentence was commuted. Monika's was confirmed. The night before she died, the Polish friends were permitted to gather in a large holding cell. Marysia Kacprzyk and Wanda Kaminska, Krystyna's colleagues from Warsaw, joined them as did an old friend from girl scout days, Wanda Wegierska, also condemned to die the next day. Wanda had been a spy and a courier who constantly travelled between Berlin and Warsaw. Her family was arrested at the same time as she was, and her mother, sister, brother and sister-in-law all died in Auschwitz. The farewell party lasted all night. They sang, recited poetry, told stories, and even played a rubber of bridge on cards Wanda had made out of cardboard. There were other prisoners in this cell as well: Poles being shipped for forced labour, and Jews from various countries. They made no objections, but respectfully moved to clear a space for the condemned and their friends.

Mimi and her fiancé, Helmut, being linked to a communist organization, had no chance of reprieve. Helmut was the first to be killed and Krystyna writes movingly about Mimi's despair and her own sense of helplessness, not being able to comfort her dearest friend. They communicated frequently, however, managing to smuggle to one another over a hundred letters and occasionally seeing one another while out for a walk in the courtyard. The night before Mimi was taken to Barnimstrasse, the administrative centre for processing prisoners either for execution or transfer, Krystyna persuaded a guard to take her to Mimi's cell for a brief farewell. Later that night, the two women climbed up on their sewing machines to reach their grated windows. As Krystyna stared into the night, she heard Mimi whistling the Polish national anthem, the clear notes filling the dark courtyard.

Parting with friends was the most painful part of prison life for Krystyna. She was overjoyed when Marysia and Wanda Kaminska were spared, especially because she felt partly responsible for their arrest since their addresses had been found at her place. Marysia wrote to another friend: "Krystyna was extremely happy that her friends had been spared the death penalty. After the trial, she hugged and kissed us with tears of joy in her eyes. She behaved as though her own verdict were unimportant. No sign of despair, sadness or regret. She proudly and very sincerely showed her happiness that her friends' lives were saved. You could see that it affected the Germans. I was proud of her and very impressed."

Olenka Jedrkiewicz's death sentence was commuted and she was sent to Witten-Annen. Her place was taken by Helena [Lena] Dobrzycka who had been arrested in Gdansk along with 43 others. Most of them were executed, but Lena was sent to Stutthof concentration camp. She managed to escape when the camp was evacuated in 1945.

Not all of Krystyna's friends at Alt-Moabit were Polish. Others, besides Mimi, included, Christiana Janeva, a Bulgarian communist and Rita Arnould, a Belgian Jew, both executed, along with a very young Frenchwoman, who was held until she reached the age of 18 before being killed.

The most exciting event at Alt-Moabit was the escape of Stefania Przybyl, a Polish woman who had *Reichsdeutsche*[2] status. She was one of many Poles living in Germany before the war who, having German citizenship, used their position to help the Polish underground. Arrested with her sister, the two were put in the same cell after their trial. Stefania had been planning her escape for some time. A tiny woman, she crawled naked through the window grate, then her sister passed her some clothing and food. With her flawless German, she talked her way out of the prison compound and escaped into Berlin where she had contacts. Her sister was executed the next day, and her mother and younger sister were arrested two days later.

Krystyna was ecstatic about this event. One letter recounts her many dreams and schemes to try the same thing. With characteristic humour, she bemoaned the size of her head which, no matter how much weight she lost, would preclude a similar escape. Instead, she was forced to endure another humiliation and hardship. Following Stefania's escape, condemned prisoners were shackled every night. Krystyna cursed her tormentors but she could not resist describing the comical aspects of the handcuffs and the oversized mitts resembling boxing gloves that were put on her and her cellmates each night.

Not much is known about the Poles who were sent to prison in Berlin. Few survived, fewer still left memoirs. Most just disappeared, last seen in the hands of the Gestapo in Poland and not heard from again. Sometimes a formal notice of execution was received by the families. Krystyna Wituska's letters offer a rare glimpse into that dark world.

We owe the existence of many of these letters to one of Krystyna's prison guards, Mrs. Hedwig Grimpe. Mrs. Grimpe had not volunteered for this job but had been assigned to it, and at times, her daughter said in a 1994 interview, she found it almost unbearable. Her presence at Alt-Moabit, however, was a great comfort to the condemned. She was good to all prisoners, but developed a special fondness for Krystyna and the other Polish women.

When Mrs. Grimpe was on duty, the prisoners could let down their guard, relax, and talk freely. She chatted with them, comforted them, brought them food, notebooks and pencils and anything else that was possible. She kept them informed about political events and military news. During air raids on Berlin, when all other guards went down to the shelters, Mrs. Grimpe stayed behind to reassure the prisoners that they would not be trapped there.

Perhaps her greatest contribution to their emotional well-being was that she enabled them to communicate with one another by delivering notes from one cell to another, and occasionally even sending some letters to their families, thereby circumventing the prison censor. All of this she did at great risk, and most remarkable of all, she involved her sixteen-year-old daughter, Helga, in these acts of kindness.

Helga became a friend, a pen-pal, whose letters brought a glimpse of the outside world to the prisoners, and to whom they could write candidly, sometimes expressing their pain and their anger, other times discussing poetry and exchanging youthful humour. At Krystyna's request, Helga copied out poetry for her—her favourites were Schiller and Goethe. This correspondence, between a teen-age daughter of a German prison guard and a young prisoner from the Polish resistance, must rank among the most unusual of prison letters. After Krystyna's closest prison friend, the German dissident Mimi Terwiel, was executed, Mrs. Grimpe established contact between Krystyna and Mimi's brother and sister, smuggling their letters into and out of Alt-Moabit.

The prisoners loved Hedwig Grimpe, whom they called *Sonnenschein*—Sunshine. Krystyna wrote to Helga about Mrs. Grimpe's appearance at the door during an air raid, how she held her and comforted her. For those few minutes, she felt she was in her own mother's arms. "Do you mind," she asked, "that I stole your mother for a while?"

Death was a steady companion to these prisoners. Every Wednesday, the inmates would be selected and taken away next day, first to Barnimstrasse, an administration centre from which prisoners from throughout Berlin were processed for their next destination—forced labour, another prison, a labour camp, a penal camp, a concentration camp, or execution. The condemned were then taken to Plotzensee, where they were beheaded.

In Poland, Krystyna explained in one of her letters to Helga, the Nazis did not bother with a facade of justice. Arrests were arbitrary and prisoners were executed on a whim, often right on the street. This, in fact, was what Krystyna expected would happen to her. But cases of suspected espionage were taken more seriously, and such prisoners were often taken to Berlin. It was an angry letter. What was going on in Berlin, she wrote, was child's play compared to the atrocities the Germans committed in Poland. What was being done to the Jews, she continued, is an unparalleled crime—ghettoization, starvation, humiliation, children smashed like dolls against stone walls, mass murder and crematoria in concentration camps—it is genocide. Krystyna was still in Warsaw in the summer of 1942 when the ghetto was liquidated. She knew about the deportations and as a member of the underground, might well have heard reports about the death camps. "Don't be surprised," she warned, "if the Poles are sharpening their knives for revenge." The next day she apologized, saying she could never hate an entire nation.

Interviewed in Germany in 1994, Helga recalled one time when her mother had to escort a young girl to her execution. She came home that day, trembling and crying that she can not go on. This must have been after the execution of Krystyna's friend, Wanda Wegierska. Before the prisoners were escorted to the guillotine, the guard had to cut their hair. Wanda told Krystyna that she would ask that her hairpins be brought back to her. Krystyna writes in one letter about a tearful *Sonnenschein* coming to her cell, bearing Wanda's hairpins. Helga also recalled the Polish women's concern for her mother's safety. On one occasion when she delivered a letter to Krystyna's cell, another guard suddenly appeared at the door. One of the girls—Helga did not remember which one—immediately stuffed it in her mouth and ate it, to protect their beloved *Sonnenschein*.

It is hard to understand why Krystyna's execution was delayed so long, almost fifteen months after sentence was passed. During that time, she went to bed every Tuesday wondering whether the next day it would be her turn. "Another Wednesday has passed," she would write to Helga. "I'm still alive."

In December 1943, Krystyna was transferred to a prison in Halle-Saale. Without *Sonnenschein* to transmit secret notes and no friends there who survived, little is known about her stay there. A German prisoner reported after the war that Krystyna was mostly in a solitary cell, and until May 1994, she was usually handcuffed. Her letters are few and quite formal—all had to pass the censor. Life there was obviously harsh, and she especially missed the companionship of Polish prisoners. Her physical condition deteriorated. In a poignant letter, she wrote home asking Zbyszek's mother, Dr. Wanda Walc, a dermatologist, if she had a remedy for her hair, which was falling out. She described herself as a "plucked chicken," said that she would remain vain until the last moment, and asked for some good shampoo.

The letters to her parents from Halle-Saale, as those before from Alexanderplatz and Alt-Moabit, are characterized by her overriding concern for them. She believed that her ordeal and death caused greater torment for them than it did for her. In this, her letters reveal a concern expressed in the prison letters of most young prisoners, both under the Germans and later the Soviets, of which there are many in archives in Poland and elsewhere in Europe. Her parting words to her mother are, "When you smile, I smile with you, but when you cry, I cry with you," and she exhorts her mother to hold her head high and to have courage, no matter what.

For the sake of her parents, Krystyna expressed hope, or at least acceptance and serenity. In her next to last letter written at Halle-Saale, she briefly entertains a futile hope that her father might be allowed one more visit, and with unexpected, spontaneous candour she writes, "I think that unlike last year, this time there would be no need to keep up appearances while deep inside we querulously wonder: will we ever see one another again?" Then, without a break, she thanks him for the hairbrush she just received.

Hundreds of Poles passed through Alt-Moabit, as did hundreds from other countries. Most died leaving no trace of their agony. Krystyna's letters are a memorial to them all. The official ones were preserved by her parents, the others were delivered to the Wituskis by Mrs. Grimpe after the war. Her daughter Helga collected her letters in an album that she called the *Kleeblatt-album*—Cloverleaf album—so named for the cloverleaf signature Krystyna, Olenka and Monika used, the three petals representing each of them. Gerd and Ursel Terwiel, Mimi's brother and sister, forwarded some others to Wanda Kiedrzynska, a historian and survivor of Ravensbruck, who first published the collection in Poland.

Finally there was Hedwig Grimpe's letter to Krystyna's parents in 1946. "I can only assure you without exaggeration what happiness I felt reading your first words to me. You lifted from me a very heavy burden." We can only surmise what the Wituskis might have said to Mrs. Grimpe, but no doubt it was in the spirit expressed by their daughter when she wrote, "I am first a human being, and only then a Pole." The Grimpes also were, first and foremost, human beings.

For Krystyna it was easier to face death believing that she would die for justice and for all humanity, and not just for her own people. With that belief she reached the universal—she belongs to us all.

[1]The eastern part of Poland was, at this time, under Soviet occupation. Germany and the USSR had, by the terms of the Molotov-Ribbentrop Pact, agreed to partition Poland. They announced that Poland had "ceased to exist" and even the name "Poland" was eradicated from their administrative communiques. Western Poland, from which the Poles, including Krystyna's family were expelled, became part of Germany and was settled by German colonists. The Soviets incorporated their zone into the USSR. The central part, simply referred to as the *Generalgouvernement*, was administered as little more than a vast penal/labour colony. All Poles had to carry identification papers including a work permit, the *Arbeitskarte,* which gave them a degree of protection against deportation to Germany for slave labour. Finding approved employment that would entitle them to this card was a priority for all Poles.

[2]German citizenship, offered to some Poles who met Nazi criteria for this status. There were many from this group at Alt-Moabit Prison.

THE PRISON LETTERS

OF

KRYSTYNA WITUSKA

Alexanderplatz Prison, Berlin
Nov. 12, 1942

Dearest Mummy,

Don't cry, I am well, in good spirits and doing fine. Things are going well. Please send me the following things: my red dress, a woollen skirt, warm underwear and stockings, a warm nightie, needles and thread, and warm slippers.

Dear Father, I beg of you, take care of Mummy.[1] She's so alone now. Please write to me often. And send me some laundry soap and toothpaste. I think about you all the time. I kiss you, dearest Mummy, and Father, a thousand times.

My address: Berlin
Polizei Gefängnis Alexanderplatz
Frauenstation V

[1] When Krystyna's parents were evicted from their home, they finally ended their disciplined but unhappy marriage. For Krystyna, the fact that her mother was alone in these circumstances was a continuous source of anguish.

Alexanderplatz Prison
Berlin,
December 22, 1942

Dear Parents,

It's almost Christmas! I send you all my best wishes and I am sure that we all have the same great wish—that some day we will be together again. I'll be thinking about you all of Christmas Day. I received two little packages from Father as well as your letters, Mummy, with all their good wishes for Christmas. I felt so happy! I want to assure you, Mummy, that I am in good health; please don't worry about me. I haven't lost weight, I haven't even had a cold. A prison doctor examined me and said my lungs are clear.[1] The slacks are wonderfully warm. The prison here has central heating and the food is much better than it was in the Warsaw prison. I can honestly say that they are polite and considerate. There is nothing to do here, though I sometimes get books or newspapers to read. We are two in the cell so I have company. My cellmate—a young German[2]—is very nice and friendly. We pass the time well enough. Since we have no lights after dark, we go to bed early.

    I am very pleased that Halina [Krystyna's sister] and her little one are well and that Janek [Krystyna's brother-in-law] is feeling better. Please send my best wishes to *Pani* Walc[3] and all her family. Please Mummy, I want you to remain cheerful and calm. We can't, after all, undo fate. I am certain we will see one another again and then I want to see you composed and in good spirits. I am very grateful to the Mierkowskis[4] for being so kind and pleasant. Don't worry if in the future I write to you less frequently. I have special permission to write three letters; that is exceptional during the interrogation period.

Please father, write to me and tell me how things are going on the Brwinów estate. Do you enjoy your work as much as ever?[5] Best wishes to all our friends for Christmas, and kisses to all.

Your Tina

Please send me a couple of 12-pfennig stamps. Our friends in Konigsberg can get them for you.

[1]Krystyna had borderline tuberculosis before the war.

[2]Rosemarie (Mimi) Terwiel, a German dissident who became Krystyna's closest friend.

[3]Dr. Wanda Walc, the mother of Krystyna's fiance, Zbyszek, who was taken to a P.O.W. camp in the fall of 1939 and at this point no one had heard from him. She will usually refer to her as *Pani* Wanda, deferential but less formal than Dr. or *Pani* Walc]

[4]Friends of the Wituskis in Warsaw, where Krystyna's mother had rented a room.

[5]Her father, an agronomist, was working on an estate in the central part of Poland, called simply the *Generalgouvernement* by the occupation forces.

Dear parents,

The day before yesterday I was overwhelmed with joy. I received a big parcel full of warm things, as well as a little package from you, Father. How did you spend Christmas? My cell mate and I spent it quite pleasantly. On Christmas Eve she received a great package from home with so many good things in it, we simply didn't know what to eat first. What's more, we had candlelight and two cigarettes. I must say, things haven't been that good in a long time. I wish you all the best for the New Year. Keep well and write often.

Things are still pretty good with me. I exercise every morning, I get something to read during the day, and we talk a lot; so it's good, all things considered—I've adapted to my situation.

Tell Halina that I'd like her to write to me about everything—especially about little Kola [Krystyna's nephew]. How I'd love to get a photo of him. Have you any news about Zbyszek [her fiancé]? I am living in the middle of Berlin, and will soon be an oldtimer here, but I still haven't seen the city. I am making progress in German, as you can tell by these letters. I am so pleased you get together with Dr. Walc quite often. She's so clever and courageous. I've always admired her.

Dear Father, why do you write so infrequently? I get mail often from Mummy but I long for news from you too.

Dearest Mummy, don't write such sad letters. Be an optimist like me, and think only about our happiness when we are finally together again. I hope you believe this as strongly as I do. Again, I send you my best wishes for the New Year. Keep well, write to me as often as possible with lots of good news.

Lots of kisses.

Your Tina

Alexanderplatz, Berlin
January 19, 1943

Dear parents,

Thank you so much for your letters and parcels. I got the postage stamps, and also those warm things you sent me. Now, dear Mummy, I'm not freezing anymore. The parcels from Father always please me and they are so useful. Are you both well? Are you very sad, Mother? I often feel guilty that because of me you are so unhappy. Don't be angry with me, dear Mummy, and try to forget about the times when I wasn't as good towards you as I should have been. I'm sorry.

Daddy, I'm sorry you have such problems at Brwinów and hope that things will get better. I do hope you can stay there. I have such fond memories of that place and love it so. I am well but sometimes, when I think about old times, I get sad. It is very comforting, dear Mummy, that you pray for me. Perhaps your prayers will not be in vain.

We cut out a beautiful cross out of cardboard and we've hung it on the window. It looks so lovely when the sun is rising, or at night when the stars are shining. Often we sit nights and gaze out the window at the sky for hours. We tell each other stories and tales and so we pass the time until at last sleep overcomes us and we go to bed. I think often about Zbyszek and I am sure his future will be bright. If you know where he is, send him the same things you've sent me. I'm sure he needs them.

Dearest Mummy, give my best wishes to *Pani* Wanda and tell her not to lose courage. Write to me a lot and often. And give my best regards to the Mierkowskis.

My darling sister, I hope that your family is all together, well and happy. How I'd love to see your little one. No doubt he is getting big and strong. Can you send me his photograph? I am so happy to think that you are together with your husband and child, living peacefully and quietly, away from life's cares. Sometimes I am jealous of you, Halinka, but I suppose I must bear my misfortune bravely.

I have one great worry and I ask your help. Please don't leave Mother alone. She is so lonely now. Be good to her. Could you not keep her with you if I must stay here much longer? Spare me this worry. Think how alone she must feel. It hurts me so much. It's only now that I'm so far away from her that I realize how much I owe her, and how I love her. I am sure you have long felt the same way and are doing everything you can to make her life a little easier.

Please raise your son in the spirit of peace. May he never be a soldier! War is so terrible and frightening.

Dear Halinka and Janek [Halinka's husband], I wish you all good things. How I'd love to be able to hold your little one and kiss him. Keep well! Love and kisses.

Tina

My most beloved Mummy,

I received your card of the 30th. The parcels will probably be returned to you, since they moved me to another prison three days ago.

These past few days I've missed you so much. I am alone in my cell and I'm having a hard time getting used to the loneliness. At least at Alexanderplatz I had the comfort of knowing that Zbyszek[1] was not far away, and I also miss the sweet and cheerful cellmate[2] I used to have. Apart from that, life here has its good side. My cell is large and warm. They've taught me how to sew on a pedal machine which is in my room and I work from breakfast until supper. In the evening I can read since we have lights until eight and we get two books a week. Before dinner, we have a little free time and we can go for a walk in the courtyard. We also have a chapel in the prison and I can attend Mass on Sunday. And the food is better here than at Alexanderplatz.

Don't worry about my health. I am well. Really, things couldn't be better than here. After all, I can write you a long letter every two weeks and tell you everything. Please give my best to Karol[3] and tell him that I never realized what a wonderful friend he was. It's so good of him to visit you from time to time. Please show him this letter, which I wrote [in German] without any help, and ask him if he's pleased with his student. I think I've told you before that I've seen Zbyszek twice. You can imagine how thrilled we were to meet; what a day that was! Give *Pani* Wanda my best and reassure her, tell her that Zbyszek will most certainly return to her.

In front of my window there are two trees, and I can see a bit of sky. In the corner of my cell there lives a little spider—he is my only companion.

Dearest Mummy, this letter would never end if I were to write all the thoughts that go through my head—this solitude will soon turn me into a philosopher.

You know something, dear Mummy, sometimes I think that life makes no sense, I am not so attached to life as I used to be. I have only one wish, and that is to cheer you up, to make you happier than you are at present. Please Mummy, be brave, hold your head high!

Tell Father that I got his letter from Brwinów and it made me very happy. Give my best regards to the Mierkowskis and to all my friends. Kisses to you and Father.

Your Tina

[1]Krystyna met her fiancé Zbyszek at Alexanderplatz. He had been arrested on charges of spying while doing forced labour in Germany.

[2]Maria (Mimi) Turwiel, the German dissident who became Krystyna's closest friend.

[3]Karol Szapiro, a young Jew from Lodz, living in Warsaw, together with his parents, under an assumed name and with forged Latvian passports. Krystyna met him when both her family and that of the Szapiros were hiding in a church residence in western Poland after that area was incorporated into the German Reich. They later met in Warsaw where the two young people fell in love.

My most beloved parents,

I've been happy all day knowing that today I would be permitted to write you a letter. These few letters are, after all, the one slender thread joining us together.

I don't know how to thank you for the parcels and letters that I received a couple of days ago. I received all the parcels addressed to Alexanderplatz. Only the one containing the pillow got lost. Dear parents, your packages give me such pleasure. How thrilled I was by the lovely dried flowers from the Polish meadow. The picture you sent me, Mummy, I've hung over my bed. Thank you for the navy blue skirt, comb and shampoo. Yesterday I washed my hair and today it is gloriously soft and shiny. Please send me more postage stamps and shampoo, otherwise I need nothing at the moment.

Dear Father, your letter made me so happy, but yet it also made me cry a little. You know, when I read such loving words, I suddenly realize what I have lost. Unfortunately, the time has passed when you could shelter me in your arms from life's terrors; I am a grown woman now and must look after myself. But I will always be brave—that I promise you—and I shall never lose hope. Never lose hope—that is my motto. I also received a card from Janek. Tell him I am very grateful. The poor idealist thinks that a new age will dawn, when people will be better and there will be no more war. I'm afraid I don't believe that.

I'm still alone in my cell, sewing blouses all day. My one

comfort is that I get beautiful books to read. Last week I got a book about Switzerland; I felt I was breathing the cool fresh air of the Alps. Now I'm reading *Théâtre de Corneille* in French. Often I think about the past—what are my friends doing—Lolek and others? Will I see them soon? When I take my walk in the yard during my free hour, I look up at the sky and I smile with joy when I see the clouds floating high above the prison walls. I feel sorry for people who are surrounded every day by even more beautiful sights but can't find joy in them, because their hearts are constricted and cold.

Pray for me, my beloved Mummy, maybe my fate will soon be settled.

Dear Father, forward this letter immediately to Warsaw[1]. Do this for me because Mummy might be worried again. I send my best regards to all my friends and I kiss and hug you with all my heart. Please, write to me often.

Your Tina

---

[1]Krystyna had to write in German to pass the prison censor. The letters went first to her father who translated them for her mother.

Alt-Moabit, Berlin,
14 March, 1943

Dearest parents,

Thank you for your letters and parcels. I got two packages from Father and three from Mummy—with shampoo, toothpaste, postage stamps and a pretty postcard. Mummy, please send me some Camelia sanitary napkins , a little mirror, my old blue silk blouse, and buy me some blue—navy blue—sandals— but make sure they're not too ugly!

Dear, kind Mummy, I feel less lonely now that I get so many loving letters from you; if only I could enclose my heart with this letter, and cheer you a little. I would love to tell you more about my situation but I am afraid to because everything was secret. You knew nothing about what I was doing because I told you nothing. Nor do you know about Military Law. It seems to be very severe. I am now in a Military (War) Court. If it is possible, perhaps you should get me a private lawyer, but this must be arranged quite quickly, if one indeed could help me. I didn't want to tell you about this before so as not to worry you, but the matter is now quite serious.

[Note to her beloved Karol Szapiro, enclosed with the letter to her parents] How delighted I was to recognize your handwriting dear, kind friend! You are for me someone from another world, someone who will soon forget about me. What am I to you, Karol? A thought, a memory? But in your world there is no time for reflection and memories. I, on the other hand, am lost in the past and like a stern judge, I examine my life. Here, in prison, one can recognize the important things in life. In freedom, one can get lost in daily cares and all kinds of details. Here we acquire some distance and so we see life as a whole. Life can only be understood if one believes in God but even then one often asks—why? Sometimes I find it so hard. You know so well how spoiled I was, how much love and understanding I demanded from everybody. Now I tell myself: can't you finally teach yourself to settle everything with God by yourself? Do you have to always have someone who will comfort and cheer you? You must learn to be independent!

When I get a letter, I want to laugh and to cry. At first I feel so close to you, and then I feel myself painfully abandoned. But letters are really the only comfort and joy. At Alexanderplatz, my friend [Mimi Terwiel] and I were so in tune. We never cried together: if one was depressed and cried—the other comforted her.

This week, I was put to work packing medicines—pleasant and light work. Spring arrives earlier here than at home. The spring shrubs are big, budding. I saw them when I was washing windows.

Dear Father, you must tell me how your work in the garden is coming along. The weather here is splendid, making this prison desert harder for me to bear.

Don't worry about my health, Mummy. That is not, at the moment, so very important. When *Pani* Wanda writes to Zbyszek, tell her to send him my love. I am sure that he is sad that we are separated again. He is still so in love with me. I am glad that your money worries are over, dear Mummy, and that things are going better for Janek. At night, in my bed, I compose endless, long letters to you in my mind. Far too long for the sheet of paper I get. You can't possibly imagine how much I love you.

I kiss you with all my heart and send my love to all my friends, especially Alina[1], Karol, and Zbyszek's family.

Your Tina

[1]Her aunt, only slightly older than Krystyna, with whom she stayed and worked in Warsaw. Alina's husband, Stanislaw Golebiowski, was killed in battle on Sept 5, 1939.

Beloved parents,

First I must thank you for your letters and parcels. Everything is delivered intact and complete, dear Mummy, don't worry about that. The parcels are opened in my presence by the *Anstaltmutter*[1], who is good to us and deserves this name.

Your packages, Mummy, are splendid and very good for the teeth. However, don't send them more than once a week. I loved the rose garland, the picture and the pretty postcards. I see that you want to keep on spoiling me, my dearest Mummy whom I love with all my heart! And from you, Father, I always get precisely what I need most.

I am healthy, serene, and working at the present time doing finishing work, by hand, on light, bright coloured dresses. We have splendid spring weather here. Only now do I understand what it means to long for one's lost country. I have everything I need here, but even a golden cage is hard on a bird accustomed to freedom. I sit and sew. Before my eyes are images of familiar places, I hear the sound of birds singing, I feel the light touch of a fresh breeze. Ahh, if only I could be there again. I can see long forgotten faces with amazing clarity, I hear their voices. My childhood and my youth are passing before my eyes, like a film. I never think about the future. But I don't want to be sad, and although I don't have a good voice, I sing all the songs I know. That helps. I pray all the time, arms outstretched, but I sometimes feel it's all for nothing. I try to think of all kinds of ways, my most beloved Mummy, how I could help you; you know, when I am sad, I tell myself that I am not alone in my sadness—that there are many people who suffer more. Think of those mothers who have lost more than one child in the war, and instead of being always lost in worry, try at least once to be one who gives comfort to others. That will make you feel so good—you'll see! I received 50 RM [*Reichsmark*] from Widzew[2]. I didn't really need them, but since I have them, I will subscribe to a newspaper, if they let me. My progress in German I owe above all to my friend [Mimi] at the Alex [Alexanderplatz]. She was a splendid, clever young woman.

Dear *Pani* Wanda. I was so pleased to get your letter. I love you very much and share your anxiety about your son. Sometimes I feel I love him like a mother. These hard trials did not weaken him, quite the contrary. He is stronger, and he has great faith—I'm sure his faith will always help him. I am convinced that his fate will be easier than mine. Please give my best to all the dear aunts and thank them for all the wonderful days I spent in Podkowa.

It was wonderful to hear from Alina. They were the first Polish words to reach me here. Have you written anything new, Alina? I am thinking now of your poem about spring. We used to say, back then, that we dreaded a boring life! Kiss your sweet children for me. I think all these things that are happening, all this human suffering, must serve some higher purpose, which we, with our human limitations, can not understand.

Beloved parents, I think it best if you don't make any great plans for my future. Better a pleasant surprise than a bitter disappointment. Mummy, please send me my blue jersey blouse, the one that doesn't need ironing.

Heartfelt hugs and kisses.

Your Tina

<hr />

[1] Literally "institution mother," the first reference to Hedwig Grimpe, the guard later called *Sonnenschein*

[2] A town in Poland. Sender unknown.

Alt-Moabit, Berlin,
11 April, 1943

Beloved parents,

I thank you with all my heart for your letters and parcels; they are my one great joy here, and a great boost for my morale. I am very grateful for your efforts to get me a lawyer; I hope that he will be able to see me soon.

I was so thrilled, my dear Mummy, to get a card from you written in Polish—what a feast! The clogs are perfect; don't worry, Mummy, everything you sent was delivered to me, including the postage stamps. I am in good health. A couple of weeks ago I told the prison doctor that I once suffered from lung disease, so he sent me to the hospital for X-rays. I haven't been informed of the results but if you wish, I can ask about it. As for my sentence, I know what it will be. I have not been in an interrogation prison for the past six months for nothing, and the Gestapo officers couldn't wait to tell me what I should expect. It's not so bad. With time, one can learn to live with any thought. What torments me most are memories of my childhood and youth, and these thoughts stay with me far into the night. I enjoy a brief respite when, between my last meal and nightfall, I immerse myself in reading, and I am overjoyed when on Mondays, I once again get two, fat books. Thanks to the money you sent me, Mummy, I get a newspaper every day. It's the *Berliner Lokal-Anzeiger*. Now I will know everything that is going on in the world. Now I must tell you a secret. I made myself a little doll out of spools of thread and I play with her. I call her Mimi— after my good friend from the Alex. No matter what you do, you need somebody. Solitude teaches one a lot, but it has its limitations. The prophets had to go into the desert in order to hear God, but they could only take this solitude for forty days. Sundays are the most boring days here. There's no mail, no work. On the other hand, nobody bothers me, and, alone in my cell, I could stand on my head if that's what I wanted to do. You know what is the most frustrating? When you're alone, you can cry, but you can't laugh. For that you absolutely need company! I once tried to laugh all by myself, but I quickly had the unpleasant sensation that I was losing my sanity.

Dear *Pani* Wanda, the Pascal Lamb[1] is so sweet. I'm at a loss for words to tell you how much pleasure it gave me. I wish I could express my gratitude and love for you in some tangible way.

No doubt you will spend Easter with Janek [Krystyna's brother-in-law] in Borowin and all the good aunts will be shaking their heads, carrying on about Zbyszek and me. Well, I wish you all a Happy Easter! I want Janek to say "Hello" to the forest for me when he goes for a walk. I miss forests and meadows more than I miss people, with the exception of course, of you, dearest parents and all my dearest friends. The happiest times of my life are associated with the beauty of nature. That is God's greatest gift to mankind, the gift of which I am now deprived. I recently got a postcard from Janek. I can see that he is overcome with love for his little son—a very happy father.

My most beloved Mummy, you must not say that I am your one joy; you still have Halinka and Kola [her sister and nephew] I love you so much, Mummy; as the war continued I always admired your courage and daring. You know, the first night after my arrest, lying not in my soft, comfortable bed but on the hard pallet in a horrible cell, I thought only of you—how will you bear this unbearable event. And later, when they were transporting me to Szucha [the Gestapo interrogation centre in Warsaw] and I saw the crowds of people on the street, happy people who glanced with such indifference at the van, I realized then that I was no longer one of them. After dark, when I can no longer read, I sit on the side of my cot but I am not really here— I am with you, in Warsaw, in Brwinów; I can see you so clearly. I used to hallucinate at first, much as you did Mummy, but in time this stopped. Could you do something special for Zbyszek? He is such a pathetic child. He worried, much as I do, that you are angry with him. Don't send me any illustrated magazines; they are forbidden. But do write more about the Mierkowskis. Are they always so good to you? What is Januszek [the Mierkowski's son] doing?

I wish you a very happy Easter and kiss you all. Give my best wishes and hugs to all my friends, especially Alina and Karol.

Your Tina

There is no problem here getting permission for visits. Unfortunately you are a little too far away, and in Berlin I have neither friends nor relatives.

[1]Pascal Lamb, an Easter religious symbol, probably an illustration on a card.

Alt-Moabit, Berlin,
25 April, 1943

Beloved parents,

No doubt by now you have been informed by our defence counsel that on April 19 I was sentenced to death for spying and for treason. I did not lose my courage, I maintained my dignity. For many long months I prepared myself for the possibility that I will have to die. My heart only aches for you, knowing how you must be suffering.

But you shouldn't lose all hope. I spoke two days ago with my lawyer who reassured me that there may be some way out of my situation and there still remains the possibility of clemency. There are still about three months left before the sentence is executed so I have time to write more than one long letter to you.

I will ask for permission to send you all the things which I will no longer need. I am so glad that the other two girls got lighter sentences. I love them both like sisters. People on the outside imagine that someone sentenced to death must go mad from fear and anguish. In fact, it's quite the contrary. Maybe that's because it's beyond comprehension. I couldn't sleep the first night and I cried a bit, but only because of you, my best and most beloved Mummy. I didn't even consider suicide—I will not take on myself the responsibility for my death.

I am not alone right now and that is wonderful. With me is a Polish woman from Warsaw who was on the same train with me to Berlin, was at the Alex the whole time I was there and now is sharing my sad fate with me. She is my age, a good,

Reichskriegsgericht
1. Senat
StPL (HLS) I 37/43
StPL (RKA) III 16/43.

Rote Liste 49/43

19. 4. 43.   0468

Geheim   26 Abdrucke.

Prüf-Nr. 0003

aus d. 21. Mai 1943

S m. geh. 1943 Nr. 43

Im Namen

des Deutschen Volkes!

Admiral

RM

28. Mai

W 445

Feldurteil.

In der Strafsache gegen

1. die Verkäuferin (Arbeiterin)
   Christine (Krystina) Ursula W i t u s k a ,
   geboren am 12. 5. 1920,
2. die Chemieschülerin Maria Zofia K a c p r z y k ,
   geboren am 2. 2. 1922,
3. die berufslose Wanda K a m i n s k a ,
   geboren am 22. 5. 1923,
   sämtlich aus Warschau,

wegen Spionage und Vorbereitung eines hochverräterischen Unternehmens
hat das Reichskriegsgericht, 1. Senat, in der Sitzung vom 19. April
1943, an der teilgenommen haben

als Richter:

   Reichskriegsgerichtsrat Lueben, Verhandlungsleiter,
   Generalleutnant Ritter von Mann,
   Generalmajor Schroth,
   Oberst Röhrs,
   Oberkriegsgerichtsrat Eichberg,

als Vertreter der Anklage:
   Oberkriegsgerichtsrat Dr. Speckhardt,

als Urkundsbeamter:
   Reichskriegsgerichtsoberinspektor Wagner,

für Recht erkannt:

Es werden verurteilt:

   die Angeklagte W i t u s k a wegen Spionage, Feindbegünstigung
und Vorbereitung zum Hochverrat zum Tode,

First page of verdict and sentence, April 19, 1943

dignified young woman. We talk all day long, we have so much to tell one another, all the things we experienced and felt while we were in solitary. We discovered that we have mutual friends in Poland; our country is so small that everybody knows everybody else. Today is Easter, the day of the Resurrection, and on this day I must write about such sad things.

We now have permission to go to church and this morning we sang in the chapel: "Gone now are the terrors of the grave. Death, where now is your victory?" I want to believe that some day we shall all be together again, that I won't be alone there where I will go. So many of my young friends will be with me: Lolo, Stas, Tomek, Zbyszek. Death is the salvation of all people and in this life I believe only in this one great truth that one sees so often etched into prison walls: "And this too shall pass." I am not afraid of death, at least no more than I would be before some serious operation; it takes, after all, just a moment—and then it's all over.

You must be brave, my best Mummy, chin up and forgive me for putting you through this. Maybe ..... maybe it will still turn out all right. There is always plenty of time for sadness.

I am also worried about Zbyszek. Better not write to him yet about what happened. He is sad enough right now. I am sure he will not grieve too long; I was for him, at most, a beautiful dream. When we were at the Alex I prepared him for the worst and he promised me that he would not be silly.

I received your huge parcel and I was so happy that I almost forgot about my death sentence; I haven't seen so many good things all at once in a long time. I look pretty much as before but I don't have much of an appetite right now and have a hard time eating what they give me.

Spring is magnificent here. The lilacs are in bloom, as are the magnolias and the chestnut trees. I finally got to see a bit of

Berlin, on my way to the *Reichskriegsgericht* [war court]. We drove past the Zoological Gardens. When you see everything bursting with life, it's impossible to think about death.

Dear Karol. So our friendship is coming to an end. I wanted so much to know how your life would unfold. You know, on the wall of my cell at the Alex someone wrote in big letters: "Everything because of your great love." So I realized that I was not really alone.

Mummy, I no longer need money, of course, just send me my navy silk dress and some shampoo. I will always be vain and I will curl my hair even on the last day. They took away my little doll. Pity, because I wanted to send her to you as a memento. We are not allowed to play here, we must only work and atone for our sins. I could, of course, still appeal for clemency; in that case maybe Daddy could remind them that back in the days when he was in Warsaw, he once saved the lives of a German family.

Once again I beg of you: hold your heads high and write often. I think of you all the time and send kisses from the bottom of my heart. I didn't get the medicines you sent, such things are forbidden.

Your Tina

Dearest, beloved Mummy, don't cry so much!

Alt-Moabit, Berlin,
9 May, 1943

Beloved parents,

I hope that the censors will not have anything against these last few letters being written in Polish. I would like you to understand them too, my dearest Mummy. I've received your wonderful, heartfelt letters. Naturally, on such an occasion I had to cry a little because I feel so terribly sorry for you and feel so guilty because I've never brought you much joy, only worries. I breathed a sigh of relief that you are not in despair and have not given up hope.

Thank you for all your words of encouragement and reassurance that you think of me. I feel very well and I am so cheerful that I feel guilty. Here I am perfectly happy while there you are all worried and thinking heavens know what. We are now three and we all have the same concerns. Olga [Jedrkiewicz] is from Warsaw and is my age, while Monika [Dymska], from Torun, is twenty-five. Olga is very beautiful and both are awfully nice. You can't imagine how wonderful it is, after a few months of solitary confinement, to once again have young friends and be able to talk as much as we like. I hardly ever think about what awaits me because I simply don't have time for that. All day long we sing, joke, and behave very much like playful girls at boarding school. We feel like we are in boarding school because there are so many things forbidden here and we're afraid we will get a scolding. All three of us have a sewing machine, Monika for making button-holes, I for hemstitching, while Olga sews very pretty dresses. At night we have to put the machines out into the corridor so we have enough room for sleeping. I sleep on the bed and they on mattresses on the floor, but they are not at all upset by that because the bed is just as hard as the floor. In any case, we sleep very well. It's the month of May, so every evening we sing hymns to our Blessed Mother, and in the daytime all the folksongs, army songs and popular songs that we know. You know, Alina [her young aunt] it is as cheerful here as it used to be in the shop.

Beloved parents, I have one final, difficult duty ahead of me, to remain brave and dignified until the end. Pray for me, dearest Mummy, that in the event that I do not get clemency and one beautiful day they take me away to the place where I will die, pray that I can do this. I didn't write my appeal until today because the lawyer said he would come to help me, but he didn't get here until now. Thank you from the bottom of my heart for all your efforts. I pray every day for God to save me, not just for myself but for you. The act of beheading lasts one second, and then I will be free of all fear and worries, but you will never be able to forget my death.

About your visit here, dearest little Mummy, I wrote a *Wunschzettel* [a list of requests] to the military court. But think about this carefully. A 10-minute visit might cause you even greater heartache. Would you not return to Warsaw even more broken-hearted? At least now, you have grown accustomed to my not being near you.

My best loved Daddy. Your brief letter revealed to me how much you think about me and how terribly worried you are about the latest news. I know that you didn't entirely realize how serious my situation was and it tore me apart whenever I had to write to you about it. I was thrilled to get all your parcels. The little bunny you sent me, Mummy, is so exquisite that I can't get enough of him and carry him about all day in the pocket of my apron. Thank you also for the pendant of good-luck charms which I divided immediately and shared with my friends.

Thank dear *Pani* Wanda and all the good aunts for their tender letter from Borowin. I truly believe that with so many good souls caring for me, nothing bad can happen to me. Do you agree now that I was right in wanting to see a lot and do a lot? Maybe I had an intuition that I didn't have much time left. Halinka finally sent me a photograph of little Kola. What a splendid, sweet little baby. I'm thrilled with him. Both photos are now on our little table. Olga made frames for them. I think that now that she has her little son, Halinka doesn't want to know about anything else in the world. She writes to me as though I were on holidays at the seashore rather than in prison. I suppose they have already sent you my watch and gold chain with the two pendants. Put the little dog [a charm] in a safe place, Mummy. I got it from a very dear person who is probably no longer alive.[1] I was to deliver it to his mother but I may never get back to Poland. Today I am terribly happy because my beloved friend, who was with me in the last jail [Mimi Turwiel] is here again. Actually, we can't be in the same cell, as before, but we see one another every day during *Freistund* [free time] and we can smile at one another. What a shame that you can never get to meet her, my beloved parents, because she is truly a magnificent woman.

I finally got permission to send home the things I no longer need, however, they said that if I decide to do that, I must send everything except what I am wearing. Therefore I decided to wait a while, until I am notified whether my verdict will be upheld, or reprieved.

Our prison days are much longer now because it is light until nine o'clock—and we say "goodnight" to one another at ten. I get up at six and as soon as I am out of bed I exercise a bit.

Olga, the pessimist, sometimes insists that there's no point in it, but I have decided to continue as always even until the last day. Then we wash from head to toe with cold water and we argue, jokingly, about who gets the wash basin first. We fold our bed linen and wipe the floor with a wet cloth. Then I prepare everything for breakfast, because I hold the position of mistress of the house, but they have to wash up after, something I've never liked doing. In the meantime, Olga and I plot all manner of mischief which ends up in such uproarious laughter that our cell is really considered the most cheerful one here.

My beloved parents, I often wish you could get a glimpse of me, at least for a moment; I am sure that would ease some of the pain in your hearts. It is pleasant now during *Freistund*, because it's warm and the four trees in the courtyard are in full leaf. Forget-me-nots, lily-of-the-valley and other wonderful things are in full bloom in the flowerbeds. If you come to visit me, Mummy, then you will see this courtyard where I walk everyday, head held high. Every two weeks we get clean towels, dishcloths and shirts. We look very funny in these shirts because they are very thick, long and so wide that I could get two of me in them. I seem lost inside, which makes Olga once again roar with laughter. That's when I think of that lovely silk lingerie Daddy gave me—what ironic fate! Now I am always wearing the navy skirt and blue jersey blouse; it is quite cool in our cell because the walls are incredibly thick and the sun peeps in only for an hour in the morning. It is dry here compared to the Alex, where it was so damp you could get stuck to the walls, and hygienic conditions in general are first rate. There are very nice bathrooms here with bathtubs where we bathe every two weeks.

Chin up! dearest Mummy, and don't worry about me. My peerless father—it's not for nothing that I am your daughter; I can bear the ups and downs of life very bravely.

I kiss you a thousand times, and all those whom I love. Little brother-in-law, Janusz, thank you for your note.

[Note in the margin] Oh, my dearest, sweetest Karol, do you know what? I am writing with the pen that you gave me for my Name Day[2]. I also used it to write my *Gnadengesuch* [appeal].

[unsigned]

[1]A present from Janek, a fellow prisoner who was in an adjacent cell at the Alex. He fell in love with Krystyna's voice. Originally from Suwalk, he was an escapee from Auschwitz, wounded in the leg during his escape. He expected a death sentence and disappeared one day without a trace.

[2]Celebrated like a birthday.

Alt-Moabit, Berlin,
23 May, 1943

Beloved parents,

I am so pleased that you have not given up hope; your letters bring me such joy! The past few days I have been extremely happy because I realized that you, dearest Mummy, are apparently the bravest of all mothers; that was the best news I could have got; I am really very proud of you. I worry that something terrible might happen to you; I received your card in which you write about the bombing of Warsaw. So long as I know that you are all right, I feel fine. We three are all getting along splendidly and we are in good health, except for poor Monika who frequently breaks out in cold sores. Not surprisingly, we are a little pale, since we never get to see the sun, and we must look like weeds that sprouted in a dark cellar. I am so pleased that you met Olenka's[1] mother. We are extremely fond of one another; we understand each other and so can be very straightforward with one another, more so than with Monika[1] who, though she is a terrific optimist, is not so cheerful as Olenka and I. Marysia and Wanda[2] are heart-warming, aren't they? Both have such strong characters and hearts of gold. Never in my life have I ever had so many friends!

Thank you so much for my birthday presents; naturally I was delighted. My birthday, despite everything, was quite pleasant; I got lots of good wishes and some presents. Olenka gave me an elephant made of coat material, a cardboard box for my letters, a bookmark, and a piece of bread. That piece of bread was the most touching because that dear person who gave it to me has a pretty good appetite herself.. Olenka and Monika sang "*Sto lat*" [a birthday song wishing one a "hundred years"]—a bit of black humour under the circumstances, I must say! We also often have all kinds of "headless dreams". All day long we sew diligently; the cell is filled with the sounds of sewing machines and our singing, we are up to our necks in brightly coloured blouses and flowered dresses. We call ourselves "Salon de mode K.O.M." [Krystyna, Olenka, Monika]

We sing a lot, a favourite is that sad song about the little eagles of Lvov whose refrain goes: "With a bleeding wound on my breast I leave you; Only for you, Mummy, only for Poland, do I grieve." Last Sunday we all went to confession and received Holy Communion. I was very upset with the news about Miodek [a young friend of Krystyna's]. You have not written for a long time about Zbyszek, Mummy. When I was interrogated about him, the police officer assured me that I would be present at his trial, so I still hope that I will see him at least one more time. I would give anything for that. The best thing for him would be to remain as long as possible at the Alex. I hope with all my heart that he will. Is *Pani* Wanda taking it well? And is Dudek [Zbyszek's brother] still in Podkowa?

Dear Alina, I think of you often and share your great anxiety.[3] Please, don't give up hope. Surely it's impossible that God would not hear your prayers. I long for the day when these dark times are behind you and your life is filled with sunshine again.

Dear Mummy, tell me, did Bruno[4] write to me after my arrest? Does he know what happened to me? We did as you suggested with the sugar, Mummy, and Olenka and I came to the conclusion that our mothers are the most imaginative. The washing powder, glycerine and shampoo are so much appreciated; we share the little pillow, each of us taking turns sleeping on it, and sometimes we toss it around and catch it like a ball. There's one thing I want to ask you. Write to me often and enclose one clean sheet of paper each time. Please send me my navy dress with the little flowers on it, it is most suitable for prison life. Also, please send a package of Camelia and a notebook and pencil—they might permit me that.

I received your package yesterday, Daddy, but I've been waiting impatiently for your letter for several days. I was so sorry I did not write to Halina in time for her birthday; I didn't think of it early enough. I am shocked by the news of the death of my dearest friend's fiancé [Helmut Himpel]. What torments me most is my helplessness; I can't go to her and comfort her. To be separated by only a few metres and not be able to speak to one another—it is so terrible. Please, Mummy, pray for her always, as you pray for me. You must write about Olenka's mother—how does she look, how does she feel? I wish I had your photograph. You know what, Mummy, ask Marysia's brother to take a picture of you; he's a marvellous photographer. And you must write to me more about your life; I find it hard to picture you because I don't know what you do all day. What's new in Brwinów? Are there guests? Karol, why aren't you writing to me? You probably don't know how to comfort me, what to say to me, but that is not at all important. As for my fate, I find myself right now in a state of complete detachment, a state I hope to maintain until the end. One's own death is not half so terrible as is the death of someone you love and that is why I feel so unbearably sad when I think of you, my beloved parents. Olenka looks quite good, though pale, and sometimes she is so lovely one can hardly take one's eyes off her.

Dearest Daddy, you must write to me because I miss you so much. I wanted to finish this letter on a humorous note but I got so upset about this terrible news [Helmut's execution] that my sense of humour abandoned me and I have used three hand-kerchiefs.

Hugs and kisses to *Pani* Wanda, all the dear aunts, Alina, Karol, and Mr. and Mrs. Mierkowski, Janusz and Leszek and you, dearest parents, I kiss most of all.

Your Tina

[1]Olenka [Olga] Jedrkiewicz and Monika Dymska, Krystyna's cell mates in cell #18.

[2]Marysia Kacprzyk and Wanda Kaminska, arrested with Krystyna.

[3]Alina's husband, Stanislaw Golembiowski, killed in the September campaign.

[4]Relationship unknown.

Alt-Moabit, Berlin,
May 30, 1943

Beloved parents,

I wonder, did you get my letter of last week, and the card for Daddy? I haven't heard from Daddy for a long time, which worries me, but I hope to hear something any day. Yesterday I got your parcel, Mummy, with the scarves and a necklace. I thank you so much, it means so much to me that you think of all these things, but we aren't allowed to wear any ornaments here. Please don't send any more food parcels either, but do send me the navy dress with the flowers.

I was so terribly upset with the news about Karol, I simply burst into tears when I got your card. My poor, sweet Karol, what could have happened to him?[1] Now that I know what it means to suffer, to be lonely, I would like to protect everyone from these things and I always pray that God will look after all my loved ones at home. I am terribly worried about you. We hear all kinds of things here about Warsaw. It is sad that you won't have darling Karol to cheer you any more, but maybe he'll still turn up! I would so grieve for him, how sad that all those from whom we could expect so much in the future are dying. Please let me know immediately if you hear something about him. In the meantime, try to comfort his mother and kiss her for me.

Did Zbyszek not write to his mother? I only know that he has been moved. How is *Pani* Wanda? Is she in good health? I am so grateful to her that she thinks of you; if only I could repay all the debts I am accumulating. Do you know what is the most painful thing about our lives here? That we know of so many human tragedies and we can't help anyone, nor even comfort anyone. We are completely powerless within these four walls, yet we feel everything. Perhaps my letter will seem very sad to you. Don't get upset, dearest Mummy, this is just momentary bitterness and then we, Olenka and I, will once again begin to sing and joke.

All three of us are well, only I don't look so good because I have been sick and in some pain, but I've been to the prison infirmary, got medication and am recovering. Monika and Olenka are indulging me terribly because of this and won't let me lift so much as a stool for fear I might tire myself. I have here in my cell your photograph, Mummy—we framed it and it's standing on our little table—now I no longer envy Olenka who has long had a photo of her mother and sister and kisses it daily. Halinka doesn't put herself out; in all these months she wrote me only one letter and a card; Remind her, Mummy, to hurry because if she doesn't think of it soon, it may be too late.

You must write to me about the bombing in Warsaw, which streets suffered most and whether any of our friends were killed; I am so interested in what is happening to you all and what your spirits are like; if only I could be there just for one hour!

I must tell you what we can see through our window: a bit of garden surrounded by a high wall behind which is an acacia, a maple, a wild lilac, and a tree we can't identify and about which we've had many arguments. One part of the garden is cultivated with a few rather miserable, prison-like flowers and 16 tomato plants (I counted them). The acacia was blooming and its scent would have reached us were it not for the smell of some rabbit cages which must be somewhere nearby. That smell brought back some childhood memories. A titmouse has a nest in the acacia and we dread the thought that the prison cat, a big white cat who makes a mess in the garden, will eat her. There's another cat here, a black one that we don't see much of, but that, Olenka claims, brings us bad luck. But in fact our window is quite high and the bottom half of the pane is frosted so we don't look out very often. The war court refused me permission to see you, so if you really want to visit, you must try to get permission from your side.

Dearest Mummy, send me a thick notebook and a pencil, which I am now allowed to have, and also another mirror because I gave mine to my friend, my dearest one for whom I asked you to pray whenever you pray for me. Daddy, maybe tomorrow I will get a letter from you; in the meantime I know from Mummy that I am in your thoughts. I kiss you both. Best regards to Alina, *Pani* Wanda, all the dear aunts, and Mr. and Mrs. Mierkowski.

Your Tina

Kisses to Olenka's mother.

[Note in the margin written by Olenka to Krystyna's mother]

Dear and cherished second Mother. Please forgive me for addressing you this way but in the month I've been with Krysia, I've come to know her so well and love her like a sister; and she has told me so much about you.

Krysia is so brave and is not at all worried about her situation believing, as we all do, that she will get clemency. She is in perfect health, and if sometimes she doesn't look too good, it is only because of prison conditions. She is always cheerful and smiling. Thank you for remembering me in dedicating a Holy Mass to us. With best wishes, Ola J. (Jedrkiewicz)

[1]Karol disappeared, at this point probably in hiding.

Beloved parents,

I wonder if you got my letter of May 23? I enclosed it with Olenka's letter to her mother but we just discovered, much to our sorrow, it was stopped by the censor because Olenka wrote about her trial, and that is forbidden. Did Daddy get my card? I am worried because you don't write to me at all, dearest Daddy. Every day I wait for a letter from you.

Here time flies at a frightening pace when one thinks that each day brings us closer to the moment when the question of our life or our death will be decided. It would please me to know as quickly as possible; I want all this behind me. We are getting on very well and we don't lose our good humour; each day is so much like another that we can't really keep track of time and I was amazed today when I realized that it's been two months since my trial. Don't worry about me, dearest Mummy, my companions are all in good health and I too am perfectly well. Thank you very much for the parcels but don't send me any more food.[1] We just have to get along without this and in fact it will ease our conscience if you didn't spend so much money on us. In previous letters I asked you, Mummy, to send me my navy print dress, Camelia, a notebook and a pencil. Your last package with the candy got here already. I don't understand why you haven't yet received my watch and chain. I was specifically called to the office in connection with this matter and I gave them your address. We are not permitted any luxuries or watches in prison so these things are kept in security. I really don't need any money, Mummy! I don't understand why you don't want me to send my things, after all why should they remain here if they could be of use in Warsaw, if not for you or Halina then for so many other needy people. You needn't worry that you will have to go to the Gestapo about this, they will simply send it to you by post.

My God, to think that I too created only problems for you and never gave you any comfort.

I came to love little Mimi, my cellmate at the Alex, so much that now I know what it means to be completely powerless to help one's loved one, to not be able to go to her and comfort her, though I know that she is unhappy and alone.

Karol's fate fills me with anxiety. Write to me immediately as soon as you hear something about him. I've received your card telling me that Zbyszek is now here at Moabit. Actually, I had hoped he would be able to stay at the Alex as long as possible, but of course his case can't go on forever. I expect that I will see him at his trial, we certainly won't be allowed to meet before then. I wrote him a note and sent it off with the hope that it would get to him. I trust that you complied with my request and didn't inform him of my sentence. I wouldn't want him to know about it before his trial. I am confident that everything will turn out better for him than it did for me, that at least he will someday return and comfort you, my beloved Mummy.

Dear Halinka. Yesterday I got your letter in which you write about your happy family and how well you are managing. It amazes us, here, so cut off from normal life, that there are places on this earth where life goes on so smoothly, happily as before. To us it seems that the whole world must be engulfed in the flames of war, that everywhere people are fighting and killing, or weeping and in agony. Lucky Halinka, may your family's nest, sheltered in a distant village, escape this unhappy fate. It seems to me that I was never intended for such a serene life, I was always drawn to extremes, and this continues, even here. No doubt you will be surprised if I tell you that I would like to live so I could continue studying and I regret terribly the time that I have wasted. Dear Olenka and I often talk far into the night, after the ever-sleepy Monika has fallen asleep, about every possible subject and we have come to the conclusion that if we were ever able to return to normal life, our outlook on life and the world would be very different from that of other people. We feel as though we are standing on a ship's plank, over the deep ocean and it's amazing that in this position instead of getting dizzy, it's quite the opposite, we are clear-headed and can evaluate everything and everybody objectively. We are no longer part of a crowd whose spirit could influence our feelings or our judgement.

Lots of kisses to you Halinka, and to Jan and the little one. And you, beloved parents, I kiss most of all and think of you always. Best regards to all those whom I love,

Your Tina

Please send me a little mirror, Mummy, because I gave mine to Mimi and please, pray for me.

[1]Most food packages were confiscated.

Alt-Moabit, Berlin,
13 June, 1943

Dear Parents!

The 11th of June was the happiest day since our imprisonment. Olenka's sentence was commuted. The Führer mercifully changed her death sentence to five years in a severe camp (*verscharfter Straflager*). We were delirious with joy, all three of us because we love one another so much, and I perhaps most of all because I have become very attached to Olenka. Now if I were reassured about my little Mimi, I would be the happiest person in Moabit. On Friday morning Olenka was summoned by the supervisor. Monika and I were terror-stricken because we assumed this meant a confirmation of the [death] sentence. We were standing in the corridor, waiting for our *Freistund*, when Olenka came down from upstairs, her little face beaming. The first day Olenka couldn't believe her good fortune. It is hard to get accustomed to the idea of life when for three months you are preparing yourself for death. I am only sorry that we will have to part because now, she won't remain here longer than a month. But that is prison life—you leave those whom you have come to love, suddenly and sometimes without even time to say good-bye.

Today is Whitsunday, we went this morning to the chapel, we got bread with margarine for breakfast, it is sunny outside, we don't have to work, so we are writing letters and reading books. Such is the holiday spirit. I imagine that crowds of people went today to Podkowa and Brwinów; those long-ago places sometimes seem so close, as though I saw them only yesterday.

Marysia [Kacprzyk] and Wanda [Kaminska] look well. Wanda will be leaving us at any moment because her sentence too has been confirmed.[1] It will be hard to say good-bye to her because she is our "golden heart." For me it is so sad because whenever someone leaves I have to tell myself that I will probably never see her again. But our good spirits never leave us, especially now, because of Olenka's good fortune. If there is anything I want to complain about, it is you, dearest parents. Daddy, you never write, and Mummy, you only send cards. If you only knew how we wait for letters, how much we worry about you and about Warsaw. I am grateful for the parcels but I have already told you in my last letter not to send me food. I only need soap, washing powder and shampoo. I will write to you more often now because the court gave me permission to do so. I feel bad that I've never had any visits: Monika had a visit from her sister, and Olenka saw a friend. It's quite stuffy in our cell now because it's quite hot outside and we can't open the window properly, though still, we are happy when the sun occasionally shines in. I wrote a note to Zbyszek.

Dearest parents, I too would like to bring you this great joy and write to you that my life has been spared. But I must be prepared for anything, that is where human strength lies, that even the worst will not break us. Our lawyer[2] quite rightly told us that hope is the source of bewilderment and confusion.

I kiss you with all my heart and please, be in good spirits as I am, and write to me. Kisses to all my friends..........

Your Tina

[1] Wanda Kaminska was sentenced to three years at Witten-Annen, a penal camp. Marysia Kacprzyk got eight years in a camp, but the prosecutor was still demanding the death penalty.

[2]Alban Rehm, a court appointed lawyer. Mrs. Wituska had contacted Albrecht Eitner, a German lawyer then in Warsaw, to ask for help in finding a defence attorney in Berlin. Eitner offered assistance to families whose relatives had fallen into the hands of the Gestapo but it was later discovered that he did this only to try to get information about the underground. At one time he served as president of the Council for the Disposition of Jewish Property. He was executed by the Polish Home Army on July 1, 1944.

[A letter smuggled to her friend Wanda Kaminska]

We should be pleased with the news of the ratification of your sentence, but I feel very sad that you will leave us, you our ray of sunshine, our little joy. I had hoped that you would go together with Marysia, and I was happy that you would be always together but instead you are leaving alone for an unknown world and your little heart will long for your friends.

I know that you do not need our advice or our instructions; just be yourself and I am sure you will find new friends who will come to love you as much as we do. Don't give up hope that you will see me again but death does not frighten me and if I must die I will die happy at least knowing that you two dearest girls have been saved.

At Zuchthous you will not be able to get news from home as you did here, but be brave, little Wanda and don't worry needlessly. I am sure you will somehow hear about our fates.

Ask Marysia to send me again, before she goes, her beautiful poems if she still has them, and pray occasionally for my poor inconsolable Rosemarie [Mimi] who can not come to terms with the loss of her beloved Helmut. Thank you again, Wanda, for your dear little heart of gold and for the sweet letter which brightened my mother's spirit.

Farewell, I kiss you a million times and wish you all good things.

Your K.

Alt-Moabit, Berlin,
20 June, 1943

Dearest parents,

In my last letters I scolded you so much for not writing, and then all of a sudden, the next week, I got three letters, two from Mummy and one from Daddy. Therefore I withdraw everything and apologize for my outburst. Your letters are such a tremendous joy to me, I am in a completely different frame of mind when I get news from you. I am the most fortunate of all three of us because I am the only one whose parents are free. Olenka is terribly worried about her mother. We try to cheer her as much as we can. I also got two parcels, one from Mummy with the dress, and one from Daddy.

I sent Daddy's parcel to a friend at the Alex because they are allowed food parcels, so nothing is wasted. Many thanks for the dress and other things; today I got all dressed up in it for chapel and looked very chic. Olenka made a lovely collar for it out of my pink slip. You have no idea how inventive we have become here; with a little patience one can create wonders out of nothing. Olenka is a true artist when it comes to handicrafts and sewing. What really pleases me is that you are so full of faith and hope about my safe return home; I no longer worry in the slightest about my situation. Yesterday, after getting our letters from home, we celebrated and laughed so loudly that we got a scolding. Prisons resemble schools in many respects, very strict schools. I received the 50 RM (*Reichsmark*) Mummy but it bothers me because there is no need to send them. I can buy stamps here. I especially want to thank you for the notebook and pencil.

If I had literary talents, I would immediately start work on a novel. It would be terribly interesting, sometimes tragic, but not without humour, which never leaves us.

Thank you, Mummy, for the news about Zbyszek. He is terribly amusing with all those plans of his for the future while we are both sitting in prison and still don't know how it will all end. Even if we were both to survive, who knows what we would do. People go through such a complete transformation in jail. Sometimes I think I am much more mature than Zbyszek even though I laugh a lot and like to fool around like a boarding school student while he is always serious. I sometimes feel that compared to him I am terribly old though here I am often asked whether I am still a minor, and when the three of us were on trial, they referred to us as *Madchenpensjonat* [boarding school girls].

I've been to the dentist, Mummy, though I didn't have a toothache, but I decided to go because of all your admonitions. Fortunately, except for one little cavity which is not yet worth drilling and filling, he found nothing. Poor Monika had to have two teeth pulled and then swelled up terribly, and she is still in pain. You see Mummy how healthy I am? I have now been eight months behind bars, and I have suffered nothing except a headache. My friends, Marysia and Wanda, don't look bad either; I saw them today in chapel. Your photograph along with my other photos were taken from me by the police when I was arrested. After the interrogation, all my papers were returned to me and they are now in safekeeping along with my other things. I am delighted that you will send me more "Lux." You have no idea how beautifully it washes one's hair, just as well as shampoo. Yesterday we all washed one another's hair and today we look like goddesses. We came to the conclusion, Olga and I, that if you are vain, nothing will change you, not even a death sentence.

Please thank Leszek[1] for his kind and heartwarming letter. How nice of him to think of me. Give my best to Mr. and Mrs. Mierkowski, and little Janusz.

I can't stop thinking about what could have happened to Karol, it's so long since there's been any news of him. It's not so difficult to find out whether someone is at Pawiak or not. [Pawiak was the main Gestapo prison in Warsaw.] And I wonder what has happened to Bruno. Perhaps he's still fighting, or maybe he has long since been killed at the front. If you should hear from him, do tell him that I haven't forgotten him. How strange life is! Give my best to Aunt Wanda and Aunt Stasia especially, and all the aunts including Mrs. Dina Korsak. They are all so lovable that I get emotional just thinking about them and I do long to see them all. Give my best regards to Mrs. Klonoska[1] and tell her that I am very touched that they remember me in their prayers. I wish them all good things. You must let me know whether my hairdresser's place has been bombed or not because he is on my list as one of the first I will visit when I get back to Warsaw, though I will never again dye my hair.

Dearest Mummy. I thank you from the bottom of my heart for all your efforts on my behalf, and when I get home, I will kiss you a million times. I will write Daddy a special card this week to thank him for his wonderful letter. We have an awful lot of work to do but otherwise we keep busy reading French and German books.

Kisses to the two Janeks and to Kola. I'd give anything for a cigarette, but that is an impossible dream.

Hugs and kisses.

Your Tina

[1]Relationship unknown

Beloved parents,

I have just received Mummy's card telling me that Daddy is coming to Berlin. I really can't believe that I will be allowed to see him and I try not to think about it because I couldn't bear the disappointment. In fact, I can't even imagine it—someone from home suddenly appearing here!

Last week we lived through a terrible ordeal. Monika and another young Polish girl left us forever. Olenka and I are both kind of stunned and can't quite believe it that Monika, who only three days ago was here with us laughing and joking, will never return again. She was so good and sweet, always thinking how she could help us or do something nice for us. And she was so sure that all three of us would somehow stay alive. I still see her dark smiling eyes. Both girls were very brave right up to the end. I will never forget our last evening together. I wish I could describe our mood, the expression in our eyes; although we all felt the dread, we were still capable of laughter, of lighthearted joking. We made plans to meet in Warsaw, though each of us knew, just as she did, that there was no hope of that. Today we only know that our girls were brave to the end.

Dearest parents, I write to you about this though I know that this will tear at your hearts, but I would like you to be prepared for the worst; it's better that way. Dear God, how I'd love to spare you this unhappiness, how I wish I could once again be a joy to you. Our cell, which used to be the most cheerful cell in the entire section, is now sad and quiet. No songs, no laughter. Monika was the mainstay of our trio, with her strong, deep voice. The last night that she was with us, we asked her to sing Schubert's "Ave Maria" for us.

Going through this together has brought me and Olenka closer than ever; we comfort one another as much as we can, and I think of our coming separation with such sadness. We have been close to one another from the very beginning. Olenka was arrested the day after I was. We were together at Pawiak, and we came to the Alex together.

You know what, Mummy, I read your letter to Marysia and Wanda, and then we read Marysia's mother's letters which are so lovely and moving that we all cried over them like babies. Do you still remember my little Mimi in your prayers, Mummy? Thank you for the shampoo, which I received unopened.

I have a great favour to ask you, Daddy. Send me a package of cigarettes and some matches. Actually we can't smoke here but just in case I must go to the place of execution, it would be nice to have one last cigarette. It would be a bit comforting, a compensation for that other difficulty.

Kisses from my raven-haired Olenka.............

[unsigned]

Alt-Moabit, Berlin,
June 1943

[Smuggled to Maria Kacprzyk]

I was so touched by your note, all the more because it was so unexpected. I only regret that we were never together, that I couldn't get to know your deepest thoughts. Marysia, how I would love to know more about you and reveal myself to you. From what I know of you, I am sure that we share similar thoughts and opinions.

Thank you for your poems, that you took the trouble to write them out again for me. You know, I had only read them once or twice when they found them during an inspection and took them away and I missed them so much. You wrote to my Mimi the things you wanted her to hear. You are very dear for remembering her in your letter to me. I loved Mimi and suffered Helmut's death with her, like the death of someone close to me. I would give anything to be with her and cheer her but I am locked up here knowing that she is suffering alone. Thank God that we [Krystyna has a cell-mate, Olenka, at this time] are still together and don't have to worry about one another. Sometimes we weave fantastic dreams of a large cell just for Polish political prisoners, where we could all be together. What a joy that would be. Not a prison but paradise! I am so attached to Olenka and the thought of her leaving makes me very sad. Together we loved to joke and act silly, behaviour that Monika [who has already been executed] looked upon with forbearance. I tease Olenka constantly and try to arouse her envy because she won't get to Plotzensee[1] and will never get to wear a black death shroud.

On this subject, we would make bets, and since earthly values no longer mattered to us, the loser would have to take the winner's place in purgatory.

I must go now, Marysia because it is rapidly getting dark but I want to copy something beautiful for you. It is an ancient German prayer that Mimi sent me. Of course, you are no longer contemplating death, dear Marysia, but this really is beautiful. Though I dream, so intensely, of life. I embrace you both, dear friends, because you are mine, and especially Lena[2] and raven-haired Wanda, because you share my fate.

> If someday I must leave
> Stay by me
> If I must suffer death
> Stay by me
> When my heart
> Is in the grip of terror
> Release me from fear
> Let Your strength, through Your fear and Your pain
> Be my shield
> My consolation in death
> Let me see Your countenance
> In Your suffering on the Cross
> Then I will gaze at You
> Full of faith
> Press You to my heart
> And so die in peace

[1] Plotzensee prison, where the executions took place.

[2] Lena Dobrzycka, also sentenced to death, later a cell mate of Krystyna's.

Dear parents,

It's now our second Sunday without Monika. How quickly times passes within these four walls of our cell. Sometimes we can't believe it. Thank you very much for your dear letters, Mummy, and for the package of washing powder, soap and shampoo. I received it unopened. Where did you get such fantastic soap? We smell it all day long and revel in its pre-war aroma. We can assume that the fact that Daddy's petition got to the Governor is a positive sign, and I am really curious what will come of it. Olenka is still with me but we are so conscious of the fact that we must soon part. I wonder who will next be brought to my cell? It is unlikely that I would be transferred to a large cell because I have the button-hole making machine here. It will be so lonely here without Olenka. Today in chapel I saw Wanda, our little "golden-heart" for the last time. She is leaving for *Straflager* [a camp] tomorrow. Little by little, our group is breaking up. Have you heard anything else about Olenka's mother?[1] She is very concerned and feels guilty because she thinks it's because of her. I feel so terrible about Karol and his parents; what will they do without him and without money? I am so pleased that things aren't too bad for you, that you, Mummy, are somehow managing. Is it true that a pair of stockings cost 800 *zloty* is Warsaw? Write to me about conditions in Warsaw, whether the cafés are always full, like they used to be?

Olenka just received letters from home, sat down in the corner on the sofa (mattress) and is engrossed in them. I hope she doesn't end up in tears, though that is what letters from home usually do. We wanted desperately to draw a picture for you to show you how I do my hair now, so that you would have a better picture of me, but after many attempts, we came to the conclusion that our drawing abilities are not up to it so I guess I will have to describe it to you. I have it rolled under, both sides ear length, and in front it is waved to the back. Do you picture it? My hair is now blond only at the ends, so if you see me again, I will look as I did long ago.

Here it is as cold as in Warsaw and I wear my skirt and blue sweater every day except Sunday, when I put on my flower-print dress. We have four camomile flowers in a glass in our cell, the first time we have such a thing in prison and it seems to us that we have never seen anything so beautiful. Where is Olenka's cousin?

I am very pleased that you have made friends. I don't want time to stand still for you, dearest Mummy. I have never needed you so much as I need you now and if I come back, then you will see how happy we will be! How is *Pani* Wanda feeling? Does she still look so terrible? Tell her not to worry about me. If only Zbyszek keeps his head about him, (and I don't doubt that he will), then I'm sure everything will somehow turn out. Marysia told me that today you will visit her mother. Marysia is really our treasure. Olenka has finished reading her letters and has fallen asleep in the corner. How lovely she looks. I must get her to lie down because she has a cold and had a fever last night. Thank you Mummy for praying for all of my beloved friends. My dear little Mimi is still here, not far away, and I see her every day during *Freistund*. I wrote Zbyszek a note but I don't know if he got it. Has he not mentioned this in his letters? Send me a bigger mirror, if you like, and also a package of Camelia. I am so curious whether Daddy will be able to come here but I don't dare dream about this, it would be such a joy. Sometimes I get very indifferent about everything, but I know I must want to live, for your sake, and for the sake of the future. Hugs to the two Janeks and to little Kola. Best regards to Mr. and Mrs. Mierkowski and the boys, *Pani* Wanda and all the aunts. I love you terribly and send great hugs and kisses.

Your Tina

Kisses from the dark-haired Olenka.

Thank you for the picture and the litany, but I don't know if I will recite it. Even prison hasn't taught me to pray long prayers, but I do believe that God does not abandon prisoners. Dear Daddy, send us some ordinary laundry soap please.

[1] Olenka's mother was arrested and sent to a concentration camp.

Alt-Moabit, Berlin,
11 July 1943

Beloved parents,

A moment ago, Olenka left me. She was transferred to the transport cell and at night, she will leave for Witten-Annen in Westphalia. I am again alone in my cell. It is so strange and so lonely. Separation is not half so hard on the one who is leaving, but for the one left behind in a place just recently filled with friendship, it is much, much harder. Yesterday we spent our last evening, keeping our tradition of singing all the songs we used to sing with Monika, we danced the polka and had a good time, but this morning we glanced sadly at one another and even our Sunday bean soup didn't taste good. One thing that pleases me is that Olenka is going to the same place Wanda went so they might meet, and then they won't feel so lonely. During my few days alone (for I hope that I will soon get another companion) I should prepare myself for the fact that I will soon be summoned by the authorities and be told what is to happen to me, and I must be prepared for everything. I still have many other matters weighing heavily upon me. Perhaps you have already heard that Marysia will have another trial which worries me terribly. My God! I was so pleased that at least all my girls [the ones arrested with her] were saved.

Zbyszek wrote me a sad letter; he fears a severe sentence. He is sure that my trial is over so he is asking me to write him the truth about everything. I don't know what to do; I'm afraid that the news will weaken his resolve just when he needs it most. Tell *Pani* Wanda that Zbyszek feels well and is calm. He used his allotted letter to write to me. I am also worried about Mimi who has a painful infection in her hand, so much that she can't sleep at night. During *Freistund*, I see the dark circles under her tired eyes but there's nothing I can do for her, only send her a kiss from a distance.

Dearest Mummy, I hope that this letter will reach you before your Name Day because I want to send you best wishes and this little handkerchief. It is so little and quite useless, but I made it thinking the whole time of you. The three flowers are symbols: yellow for Olenka, red for Monika, and blue for myself. Don't worry about a thing, Mummy and I love you for writing to me so often. Catholic services are held in the prison chapel, on the fourth floor, every second Sunday. Everybody attends if they have permission from the court. I have had permission since about Easter, and some other girls have too. Beloved Daddy, you can't imagine how enthusiastically I greet your letters, each of which is guaranteed to improve my humour for at least two days. The last one was no exception and I eagerly await the promised parcel. I will try to send you a card mid-week. I am sending you excerpts from a poem written for us by an unknown author.[1]

Three little Polish children
Ever cheerful and serene
Live in cell no. 18
Berlin, Alt-Moabit.
Fate united them
Far from home and native land
They never complain
They are so brave.
They served their Polish homeland
With the best they had to offer,
They took away their freedom

And now they want their lives!
Olga's sentence was commuted
With boundless joy they thanked God
for showing his love
But one had to die—little Monika
She who was most convinced
That freedom was near.
A profound silence descended
Where once there was singing and dancing.
Soon Olga too will leave
Then Krystyna will wait all alone.
Dear God! grant her life
I will be eternally grateful.

I hope this poem will show you that we maintain a positive mood and spirit no matter what fate demands of us. Write to me, Daddy, and tell me what sort of harvest you expect this year, not only in Brwinów but everywhere. How I'd love to walk with you through the fields. Here I can't even stick my head out of the window because the bars are too close.

Kisses to you both, with special Name Day kisses for Mummy, and kindest regards to all my friends.

Your Tina

Mummy, send me my new stockings which I left in the cupboard.

¹Mimi Turwiel. Not clear why she is not identified.

Alt-Moabit, Berlin,
24 July 1943

My own, beloved Mummy,

Today is my Name Day so I am sure you were thinking all day about your little girl, so far away. This morning, while I was still sleeping, Lena [Helena Dobrzycka, Krystyna's new cell mate] put your photograph on the pillow near my head, and all day it seemed to me that you were here with me. I got your package today, just after dinner and I thank you so much for all those lovely surprises. I immediately sewed a dress for my naked little doll and I won't part with it for a moment. Lenka [Lena] made a handkerchief for me, embroidered with every natural and supernatural symbol of good luck, which should protect me from death!

But the finest Name Day present was the happy outcome of Marysia's trial. For several weeks, since we first heard about her re-trial, I lived in a constant state of anxiety. I only found out on the morning of her trial that I too would have to go, to testify. Naturally, we were ecstatic, first of all because it is always better to go together, and that also meant that I would not have to wait to learn the outcome. I wasn't there for the whole thing, only at the very beginning and then I was recalled for a few minutes to testify. The rest of the time I was in the *Arestzelle*, where prisoners wait, guarded by soldiers. You can imagine how nervous I was. I thought it would never end, though in fact it lasted three and a half hours. I caught a glimpse of Marysia returning through the courtyard. She was smiling, so I decided that things went well. On our way back, we looked so happy that our guards asked us if we were *freigesprochen* [acquitted]. They were absolutely amazed when I told them that in three months time I will be executed. I am so pleased, and it is so much easier to accept my sentence, knowing that my girls will return home.

Mummy, try to see Olenka's sister or grandmother and ask them if they have any news of her from the camp. If they can write to her, ask them to send her a kiss from me and tell them about the fortunate outcome of Marysia's trial. They should also tell her that we are now three in cell no. 18, that everything is fine except that I miss her so much. You probably don't know who Lena is and what a wonderful friend I have found in this jail. Lena spent a few months in Lomianki with her aunt and uncle Makolski, and there she was arrested last summer. This came up in our conversation just by chance. Now we are both awaiting the results of our appeals—Lena has been waiting almost six months.

Is that Daddy of mine going to come to visit? Because a lawyer came to see Marysia today and told her that her father got his permit and will soon visit her. So I got very jealous, especially since Marysia is bound to see her father some day anyway. Last Sunday was wonderful. I got such sweet letters from *Pani* Wanda, aunt Bronka and Alina, and I was especially pleased to hear about you, Mummy, that you are so fantastically courageous. I am so grateful for that, my dearest Mummy. You must persuade the two Janeks to come to you; it would be safer for them and better for you.

Pani Wanda wondered how these experiences will affect our character and disposition. It is hard to evaluate that here, under these abnormal circumstances. We will only know once we are out again in a normal world. We too have discussed this, whether we will ever be able to live again like normal people. We think we will see the world through different eyes because here, living with a death sentence hanging over us, so many things have become unimportant. Anyway, we decided that when we get out we will be very fussy about choosing a husband. It can't be just anybody because few men will impress us; we have endured and learned so much.

You know, Mummy, here it is a fact that women take death sentences much more bravely, that they bear all difficulties with much more dignity, and so I am a bit conceited. But not too much.

I wrote to Zbyszek last week and I was a bit relieved to hear from *Pani* Wanda that there is some hope for him.

25 June 1943

[letter continued]

Back to my letter. Today is a terribly boring Sunday, we don't go to chapel or to *Freistund*, in other words we sit all day in our cell and we don't even work. Outside the weather is glorious and hot—in the cell it is so hot we can't breathe. The best moment is when we can cool off a little by washing from head to toe in cold water.

I rather hope that today I will get a letter from you for my Name Day because all I got this week was a brief note. Write to me, Mummy, and tell me what Jacek is doing, and whether he is still pessimistic about the whole world and the future? How is little Eva. Give Kasia my best and tell her to get well soon. I am so pleased that you have good friends who can comfort you.

I want to thank you, from Mimi, that you pray for her. Actually, she is a full ten years older than I, but very delicate and looks almost like a child. Her mother doesn't know she has been arrested and sentenced to death. She has a heart condition, so Mimi's brother and sister are keeping it from her, telling her that Mimi has gone to Switzerland. Consequently, Mimi gets no letters from her and misses her terribly. I am luckier in that respect and feel very sorry for her. I am getting along very well with my new cellmates but Olenka was my favourite of the Polish girls here. Lena and I keep asking ourselves just how long we will remain together. Marysia has met several times with our lawyer who reassured her about our situation though he hastened to add that fate does play tricks. But don't fret about this, dearest Mummy, just keep your chin up, as I do. There's lots of time for worrying, I always tell myself, and I enjoy every day as much as possible.

Kisses from the bottom of my heart, my one and only Mummy and thank you again for the letters and parcels.

Your Tina

[Note to Aunt Alina]

Dearest Alina—Your postcards are beautiful. Often in the evening I remove them from the box, set them on the table and gaze at them. What a beautiful, incredible world they show, so different from ours. One simply forgets that somewhere there are silent, peaceful evenings. Last night Marysia woke me up to look out at the moon which appeared through the grill, high above the prison walls.

Hugs to you and your darling babies and thanks for all your prayers. I too think of Stan. [Alina's husband, killed at the start of the war.]

Your Tina

Alt-Moabit, Berlin,
1 August 1943

[Smuggled letter to Helga, the teen-aged daughter of Hedwig Grimpe, the guard they called *Sonnenschein*.]

Dear little Helga,

We were so moved that you sent us some apples! We were as disappointed as you that you couldn't come to us yesterday. You have no idea how much it means that someone is good and kind to us. Unfortunately, not all the guards are as nice as your mother. We call your mother our "ray of sunshine" and are so happy when we see her. She just brought me a blouse for buttonholes and I set to work with such zeal that I broke the needle.

Little Helga! You are a girl from another world, the kind we have almost forgotten, where girls live with their mothers and can come and go as they like. You can see and hear beautiful things, but we are surrounded by grey walls and all our thoughts about the future end with this question —will I live to the end of this week? Still, we try not to lose our good humour, to maintain good cheer—as much as we can. We tell ourselves this is not a prison but a strict boarding school and our guards are our horrible teachers. Only we miss our country and life is sometimes unbearable thinking about our mothers who await with dread the final outcome of our appeal.

It's too bad you can't come here in the evening and stay a while. We would sing you our songs and tell you about our experiences. Many old people have not lived through as much as we have. We feel optimistic today and talk about being out and going to a café with our little friend Helga. We would eat cakes until we almost burst, and on top of that I would chain-smoke ten cigarettes.

Don't laugh at my faulty German but I only studied it during the war. All the best from the three of us.

Krystyna, Maria, Lenka

I am enclosing two addresses, one in Warsaw and the other for our estate where we hope to return after the war. One of these is sure to be good but try the one in Warsaw first.

Krystyna Wituska
63b Wspolna Street, apt 5
Warsaw

or

K. Wituska
Malyn Post Office
Majatek Jerzew, Poland

[smuggled letter]

Dear Helga,

The apples were delicious. We gobbled them up very quickly for fear of getting caught, and destroyed your letter immediately. *Essigsaure Tonerde*—Acetate Slime—isn't that a fantastic nickname.[1] We racked our brains for the longest time and nothing could be more appropriate. From now on we shall never call her anything else, but you can imagine how careful we must be. They're always eavesdropping. She spies on us all the time and once said to me: "If I had a daughter like you, I would go crazy." Thank God, I thought, that she has no children. They would be tormented mercilessly.

Your letter helped ease the deep sorrow which has enveloped us since yesterday. Yesterday my dearest friend [Mimi] who was in my cell for a long time at the Alex, was taken away to Barminstrasse. She was sentenced to death six months ago so I am so afraid for her, and what depresses me most is that there is no way to find out whether she is still alive or not.

Do the air raids frighten you, Helga? Won't you get away from Berlin during this dangerous time? To enable us to protect ourselves in the event of an American bomb hitting here, we now get our washbasin and food bowl filled with water every evening. [Presumably the water was supplied in case of fire though clearly Krystyna saw how ridiculous it was to think a bowl of water would put out a fire caused by a bomb.]

„Essigsaure Tonerde"

Drawing of hated prison guard that Krystyna and her friends
called Essigsaure Tonerde, or Acetate Slime.

On Sunday we saw your beautiful dress. We think you will look splendid when you step out.

If it weren't for my anxiety for my friend, we would be feeling quite good right now, but even when things are bad we never show it. No one here must ever so much as think that they have defeated us.

My sentence has still not been ratified (touch wood three times!) It would be terrible to get killed just before the end of the war. I have to stop now, Helga, before the guard notices that my sewing machine is silent. How awful it is to know that I can be observed at any time through the peep-hole. Unfortunately, most of the time they are not your mother's eyes but those of the other "aunties" [nickname for all the guards], peering into our cell lest we be doing something forbidden. Once again, thank you and best regards

Krystyna W.

[1]A hated guard.

[smuggled letter]

Dear little Helga,

Despite the rain outside, we had a bright day here. *Sonnenschein* dropped in several times and on her last visit, she brought your letter and some marvellous apples. You know, as soon as I'm out of here, I will invite you to Poland, where my parents have a large estate with lots and lots of fruit trees. You see how nervy I am—a death sentence hanging over my head and I plan for the future. You know what else we like to do when we are on our pallets? We plot our escape! If only we had a file to cut the bars on the window etc. We picture the look on the face of the guard when she walked in and found the cell empty and the thought of it makes us laugh. For the time being, however, we are very much stuck here. It is still light outside but here it is "evening," since we ate supper long ago (gloppy cereal). I never fail to be impressed by your lovely writing paper—I'm so used to using just any scrap of paper.

Are you feeling better, Helga? *Sonnenschein* told us you weren't well and couldn't sleep last night. I too can't sleep but for a different reason. I'm so worried about my friend. If only I knew if she is still alive?!

What's a planetarium? I don't know that word. It must be something wonderful since you want to take me there. I can't find the rabbit—it must be a joke, just to catch people [probably referring to some kind of a riddle-drawing]

Best regards from your Krysia, Marysia and Lena

Alt-Moabit, Berlin,
10 August 1943

Beloved little Mummy,

Today I got your card dated July 27 and the parcel containing cotton-wool and a pretty collar. Please don't send me any food because that causes more harm than good. Besides, that's really not important, I'm not hungry anyway. I'm sure you were worried because I hadn't written for so long but a lot happened last week and I had a hard time collecting my thoughts. You must have heard the good news about Zbyszek's verdict. I can imagine *Pani* Wanda's happiness, much as mine. Two days after his trial we met and could talk a little longer. Zbyszek was beaming with joy and I was happy to see that he looked quite well, which he certainly didn't at the Alex. He was also quite pleased with how I looked.

Mummy, they took my little Mimi away and I don't know where but I suspect the worst. If you knew how much I came to love her you would realize how much this hurts me. Anyway, no matter what, we must hold our heads high, just like Mimi did, to the end!

Stay calm, dear little Mummy, I am really not afraid. If only I could reassure you somehow. Thank everyone in Borowin for the card they sent me on my Name Day. It was so sweet of them. Kisses to *Pani* Wanda and Alina, and regards to Mr. and Mrs. Mierkowski. And most of all, a kiss for you, my best Mummy.

Your Tina

[smuggled letter]

Dear Helga,

This will be my last letter to you for now because *Sonnenschein* is leaving us for a while. Will there ever be another good week like this one? We will feel like orphans. I wonder what kind of witch will replace her? You are a sweet girl, Helga and your letter saved me from a flood of tears; *Sonnenschein* told me that Mimi was dead. It's better that I know though it will be very hard for me to get used this thought and I will never get over this loss. I console myself that Mimi is no longer suffering. What a shame, a terrible shame, that such a good, talented human being had to die such a horrible death.

You probably know that we got lots of mail today, including the news that my father received permission for a 15-minute visit. I'm so afraid that I will get too emotional and not be able to say a word. After all, I must show him I am brave and up to any situation. They are already suffering too much.

Pity that the idea of the gramophone is impossible. We miss music so much. Yesterday we could hear someone playing a piano; we sat motionless, deeply moved. Where did it come from? At that moment I realized how much of the world's beauty has been taken away from us.

Your letter from the air raid shelter was so shocking. It's much easier for us. We are ordered to get dressed but since it's completely dark and nobody can see anything, we might, at best, put on a skirt and calmly go back to sleep. We only regret that we must black-out our windows because it would be interesting—bright rockets and colourful bombs.

I will ask for the book that you want on Monday (our book day). I will probably be able to get it. The weather is getting nicer. I'm sure you will be able to enjoy some fresh air on Sunday. If they take me away, Helga, I will write one last letter to you. I will leave it with Maria if *Sonnenschein* is not here. And when they have killed me, I will float like a fat little angel on a cloud above your house to see what you are doing. We are very careful with the letters Helga, because we know how dangerous it is for your mother. I will tell you a secret. Mimi and I exchanged more than 200 letters without getting caught. Prisoners are so carefully watched, and yet still find ways to communicate. The guards are cunning, so we are more cunning—that is our motto. Before inspections, we hide everything so well that even we can't find it later.

Good night, Helga, It's completely dark now and we have no lights. All the best,

Your Krystyna

[letter smuggled to Helga]

Hello!

Sonnenschein told us what happened last night. What a loss. I am so sorry, and furious, that this happened to your mother. [Mrs Grimpe was robbed during an air-raid.] She's so sweet though, that despite everything, she still brought us a bag of tomatoes and apples. Let's hope that your things are recovered. Through our window we see only a bit of sky, however it's enough for us to observe all sorts of wonderful clouds. Often I stand by the window, gaze at the sky, and long for freedom. I select for myself a special cloud. Helga, you are your mother's greatest treasure. Because she has you, all her sorrows are bearable. Stay as lovable as you are.

Your Krystyna

Alt-Moabit, Berlin,
15 August 1943

My dearest Mummy,

Yesterday I got your letter, scolding me for not writing for such a long time and wondering whether a letter of mine had been confiscated by the censors. It's just that last Sunday, I wrote to Mimi's brother and sister, and the Sunday before to Zbyszek.[1] You and *Pani* Wanda must be so happy about Zbyszek's verdict; what good fortune. I didn't even dare dream it could turn out this way. I saw him that day; such a pleasant surprise but that was also the day Mimi left us, so I had to force myself to appear in good humour. Mimi is gone forever, like the other girls. The only comfort is that all the evil things are behind her now; she will no longer suffer and long for her beloved Helmut. Now I finally realize what it means to lose someone you love, forever! I also got a card from Daddy yesterday and he writes about visiting me soon. I am delirious with joy but I am still afraid to believe it, I can't believe it is really possible. But now I will wait for this every day. We heard from little Wanda from *Straflager*; she is with Olenka and their work is hard but clean. It is a camp for Polish women only and there are 72 of them. I gather from their letter that they are not doing too badly. It would be good if Marysia were sent there too. You must know that she is in my cell, along with Lenka Dobrzycka about whom you've probably heard from Mrs. Makolska—if you get to see her. Both of them look well and are in good health. I am now sort of a *Stubenalteste* [head girl in the cell] because I speak German best and I feel like the oldest, though in fact there is no difference in age between

Lena and me. Halinka is awful for not wanting to be with you[2] although, who knows, under the circumstances, maybe I too would prefer to stay with my husband, if I loved him. At this moment, I just got your letter dated the 2nd, in which you write about Olenka. Thank *Pani* Wanda for her card. Perhaps I will write her a few words but at the moment I don't feel up to writing a letter. Forgive me, but I must finish now.

I love you and thank you for writing so often. Give my best to everyone.....

Your Tina.

[1]Krystyna was permitted only one letter per week.

[2]She wanted her sister to move to Warsaw so their mother would not be alone. No doubt Halinka remained in the country with her small child because it was safer.

Alt-Moabit, Berlin
August 17, 1943
Gelesen: _____
To be signed by: *Sonnenschein*

[This smuggled letter to Helga was written on official prison stationery so
the instruction for *Sonnenschein*'s signature is a joke. "Gelesen" —"Read by,"
is the space for the censor's name.]

Dear Helga,

Today was, without question, the most unbelievably happy
day. My head still can't fully absorb the fact that today I actually
saw my father. Looking at him sitting across from me, I felt that
my year in prison and my death sentence were just a bad dream.
I managed to maintain my happy disposition the whole time he
was here, Helga, and I am sure that my father left me convinced
that I am getting along here very well. He even managed to
exchange a few words with our *Sonnenschein*, and that reassured
him that I am getting good care here. Unfortunately, they took
away the sweets, the cigarettes and the flowers he brought me.
But that doesn't matter! During our conversation, he expressed
the hope that before too long we will be able to return to our
family estate in Wartheland, our home from which the Germans
evicted us. But it is not the estate that is important, but only
that we are all together at last. I gave him Mimi's family's address
and asked him to go see them and give them my kindest regards.
The only thing, it was such a short visit and there was so much
to say. I want to believe that someday I will be able to tell him
about everything. And, oh, I was able to hug him! How comforting that was.

Later in the afternoon I had a visit from our lawyer, a totally

Name des Briefschreibers:

Christina W.

Zug.-Nr.: ???? !!!

(Bei allen Sendungen anzugeben)

Berlin NW 40, den 1?. August 1943
Alt-Moabit 12a

Gelesen: _____

(Hier muss Sonnenschein
unterschreiben)

Liebe Helga! Du weisst es schon, heute war ein ausgesprochener
Glückstag! Ich kann noch nicht richtig begreifen, dass ich
meinen lieben Vati gesehen habe. Als er mich so gegenüber
sass, hatte ich ein Gefühl, als ob das ganze Jahr hier
im Gefängnis u. die Todesstrafe nur ein nächtlicher
Spuck wäre. Ich habe es geschaft Helga, ich war die
ganze Zeit so guter Laune, dass er mit der Gewissheit
weggegangen ist, es gehte mir wirklich glänzend.
Das war auch prima, dass er mit unserem Sonnenschein
die paar Worte wechseln konnte, jetzt ist er auch
ruhig, dass ich gut behandelt sei. Leider musste er
alle leckeren Sachen, Zigaretten u. den Blumenstrauss
welchen er mir mitgebracht hat gleich bei dem Eingang
lassen, aber das ist Nebensache! Er hat bei der
Sprechstunde seine Hoffnung geäussert, dass wir bald
auf unseres Familiengut in Wartheland zurückkehren
werden, aus welchem uns die Deutschen rausgeschmissen
haben! Aber auch das Gut ist gar nicht richtig, wenn
wir wieder alle zusammen sind! Ich habe ihm auch

C 2001

pointless visit. He lectured me a lot about hope and apologized for not greeting me during Maria's trial but it is forbidden to communicate with people sentenced to death. What a laugh! I told him so.

Now about your letter: You are a marvellous girl. We positively cheered on discovering that you think as we do. You know, I practically faint when I read in the newspapers about "holy hatred" and revenge—against me, I suppose, since I am one of the enemies of the Reich who must be liquidated. So they must get their revenge by cutting off my head! I sometimes think that they won't grant me clemency simply because things are going quite badly for them, so they'll think they can't afford the luxury of being so magnanimous. I don't care! Dear, dear Helga, I am sorry if I've made you unhappy with my letter. I didn't mean to. We *Kleeblatter*[1] are so used to talking about death, we think it's a perfectly natural, normal topic for conversation. I forget that for others, it might be depressing. In fact, today my pleasant neighbour and I carried on a great philosophical discussion of precisely this topic during our daily walk. The guard was gracious enough not to disturb us.

Yesterday, a cigarette fell from the heavens. I smoked it in the evening. To be honest, it made me feel a little ill, it's been so long since I've had one. But it was splendid!

I have to stop now because it's getting too dark. But I'm too agitated to fall asleep—my father is still in Berlin. His train leaves at eleven.

Lena and Maria send their thanks for your kind words and we all wish you and our *Sonnenschein* a peaceful night, without air raids.

Best regards from your *Kleeblatt*.

[Note in the margin]

Hello again. Just a few words while waiting for *Sonnenschein* to come. We still have the little dog [a mascot made out of rags]. He has such a funny expression on his face, we can't help but laugh. My wish that you would have a night without an air raid, alas, did not come true.

[1]*Kleeblatt*, meaning Cloverleaf, was Krystyna's symbol for herself and her two cellmates, Marysia and Lena. Sometimes instead of signing off with her name, Krystyna drew a cloverleaf, with each one's initials in each of the three petals. Helga collected all their letters and drawings in an album which she called the *Kleeblattalbum*. It is now in the archives of the Main Commission for the Investigation of Crimes Against the Polish Nation, in Warsaw.

Dearest Father,

I hope you returned home in good health and in good spirits. Now you no longer have to worry, having seen for yourself how well I'm doing. The person [*Sonnenschein*] whom you chanced to see is very sweet and lovable. Pity you couldn't speak to her. I am very curious—did you get a chance to meet and speak to Gerd and Ursel [Gerd and Ursel are Mimi Terwiel's brother and sister], and do they know yet what happened to Mimi? Are they grieving terribly? You absolutely must write and tell me everything. I loved that girl so much. She was the best companion imaginable—so gifted, good humoured and always ready to help others. I'd like to have a sister like that. Losing Mimi has been a terrible blow for me.

Our court-appointed lawyer was here yesterday and gave me a long lecture about hope. All day I've been in high spirits and people were admiring my radiant face.

You are a wonderful person. Despite all your difficulties, you got here. Too bad I couldn't keep the cigarettes and the sweets—but that is not important. The main thing, I always say, is my mental state. Keep well, and bravely hold your head high, no matter what happens.

Heartfelt kisses to you both, and to Michael.

Your Tina

Alt-Moabit, Berlin
18 August 1943

[smuggled letter]

Dear Helga,

In your letter you mentioned *Sonnenschein*'s fattening treatment. You know, I'm worried that if this keeps up, I will lose my slender silhouette! When I was at the Alex with Mimi, we really starved so it's no wonder that I'm not fat. How overjoyed we were when one of the cleaning women, who couldn't chew because of her dentures, took pity on us and gave us her bread crusts. Still, despite the hunger and the cold at the Alex, I remember those days as a special time. Mimi and I were together in a tiny cell and, just to spite them, we laughed constantly. Tonight, if I have time, I will tell you more about our life at the Alex. I didn't get the books. They gave me three books that I've already read. My father is now in Warsaw.

All the best—your Krystyna.

18 August 1943

[smuggled letter]

Dear Helga,

Sonnenschein just came in to say goodnight and once again brought us some splendid cakes. Helga, you have no idea what a golden heart your mother has. You'll never understand how much her dear heart—not to mention those cakes!—mean to us.

We now have a new guard, an awful, blonde woman and all day long we hear her resounding voice bellowing in the corridors. We call her *Bazyliszek*, the name of a dragon in a children's story who could kill just with his glance. She really does have the most horrible eyes. When we are out for our walk, we must look straight ahead and we can't smile, or else she sends us immediately back to our cell. She is always very self-important—must be working for a promotion.

Today, right after supper, I heard a victorious cry from the neighbouring cell: "The army has retreated from Sicily!" Unfortunately, we had no champagne, only water, or else I would have got royally drunk—to ease our sorrow, of course.

What a shame that Mimi is not here to hear this. Now I must tell you something about the Alex. The cells were very small with only a narrow cot and a stool. Nothing else; in any case there was no room left for anything. We sat all day on the cot, wrapped in a blanket. It was terribly cold; they never heated the place. We had to sleep together on the one cot; it was uncomfortable but it kept us a bit warmer. We had to share the bed with a great extended family of bedbugs. The walls were wet and sticky. Nobody cared about us and we could have died three times before anyone would notice we had hoisted a flag. [They kept a Polish flag hidden under the cot.] But it was better that way. At least we were left in peace. We could have hidden a machine gun under our beds; our cell was so lice infested, none of the guards ever stepped inside. There were no inspections. We could stand all day at the windows and talk to our neighbours. Although that wasn't so easy since only the top ventilator was open. We had to balance on our toes on the edge of the window in order to get our heads out. After a while, I got used to this unusual posture and could hang there for hours—except after supper when I'd get a belly like Buddha's, in which case I'd soon feel quite ill. We had a fantastic postal service organized there. Using a long pole to open the ventilators, we passed along books, newspapers, cigarettes, bread, even bowls of soup. The windows were so close together that it was quite easy to reach. We also established contact with the men, who were on the floor below us. Using a rope, we managed to lower bowls of soup since the Gestapo often deprived them of it. Sometimes a tragedy—the string broke and everything landed on the ground in the courtyard below. What a loss for a starving man. When we had no string, we tied our stockings and handkerchiefs together. All this was done after dark. We lived on the fifth floor. Sometimes, when we shouted from one window to another, Schup would call out from the courtyard, "Quiet up there!" And everything would be quiet for five minutes.

To be continued. It's dark again. All the best, your

wagte sich in die Zelle, sie fürchtete die Wanzen u. Läuse. Wir hatten nie 'Revision gehabt. Den ganzen Tag konnten wir am Fenster stehen u. mit unseren Nachbarn plaudern. Das war auch keine leichte Aufgabe, weil wir nur den Oberlüft offen hatten u. wir mussten auf die Zehenspitzen auf dem Fensterrand stehen um den Kopf draussenstecken zu können. Mit der Zeit habe ich mich auch an diese ungewöhnliche Position gewöhnt, u. ich konnte stundenlang so hängen, nur nach dem Mittagessen nicht, wenn ich einen Budda- bauch hatte. In diesem Fall war mir sehr schnell übel. Wir hatten dort eine fabelhafe Postorganisation. Wir schickten uns von Zelle zu Zelle mit der Hilfe eines Fensterstockes Bücher, Zeitungen, Zigaretten, Brot auch Töpfe mit Suppe. Die Fenster waren so nahe, das man ganz gut reichen konnte. Wir hatten Verbindung mit den Männer die unter uns sassen, wir schickten ihnen Suppe auf einer Schnur unter, weil sie oft kein Mittag bekamen auf Befehl der Gestapo Komissaren. Es passierte manchmal ein Unglück u. die Schnur brach u. die ganze Ladung landete auf den Hof. Das war sehr bitter, für den, der Hunger hatte u. auf seine Portion wartete. Wenn wir keine Schnur hatten, banden wir unsere Strümpfe u. Handtücher zusammen. u. das mussten wir alles in der Dunkelheit schaffen. Wir wohnten auf der fünften Etage, wenn wir sehr laut von Fenster zu Fenster schrien kam manchmal ein Schupo auf den Hof und brüllte — Ruhe da oben! Dann waren wir 5 Minuten still.

Fortsetzung folgt.

Es ist wieder dunkel!

Herzliche Grüsse
Dein.

Alt-Moabit, Berlin
[sometime after 19 August 1943]

[smuggled letter]

Dear Helga,

I am sure you've spent a pleasant Sunday with your Mummy. We are delighted with your letters from Turingen; it's nice of you not to forget us even while you're away. We laughed at your Nazi "friend." Today we're hungry like wolves. I've searched the cell but there's nothing here apart from soap and toothpaste. Pity. You'd better wait until I've finished telling you my story before you decide whether you'd like to join us. My friendship with Mimi was the bright light of my miserable prison life; everybody who knew her will not easily forget her. She was splendid, so talented, good humoured and always ready to help others. She was a lawyer and very musical. They couldn't break her.

At the Alex, after she was sentenced to death, Gestapo officers frequently appeared at the cell to say they were coming to take her to Plotzensee.[1] Maniacs that they were, they thought this was a joke—they wanted the pleasure of frightening her. But she never reacted and each time they left sorely disappointed. It was here, at Moabit, that she finally became very depressed, when they took away her fiancé. She loved him terribly and—something rare—he was worthy of her love. That's when I really worried about her, that in her grief, she might do something. I was the only one who knew what she was going through at this time. Whenever she went out of the cell, it was always with a smile. She was too proud to reveal her pain. I often ask myself:

What will happen to a nation that murders its best people?

I'm afraid that this letter will depress you again, but it is impossible to write only cheerful letters from a prison. Besides, you said I could express whatever I feel. I don't think one should know only pleasant things; one must know everything that is going on. Not many people in Berlin realize how many men and women are confined in these cells, how many executions are carried out each day. We are once again in shock—seven French and Belgian women, among them Mimi's friend [Rita Arnould, a Belgian Jew] were taken away to *Barminstrasse*.[2]

You know, you're right, Marysia [Kacprzyk] is a melancholy girl. I worry about her and will be relieved when she is taken out of here and sent to the penal camp.

On Saturday, we got the most wonderful surprise. Our sweet, cheerful neighbour (Jutta) was sentenced to only eight years in prison. She expected a death sentence. An absolute miracle! She has a five-year old daughter, and dark, laughing eyes.

Do you know how to tap dance, Helga? I learned it in jail. In Alexanderplatz, where we could barely move a few steps, Mimi gave me tap dancing lessons. Of course that only made us hungrier, but at least we didn't freeze. Ivan, the Ukrainian below us, nearly went mad from the noise of our exercises. Two cells away was a dancer who also exercised a lot. She was very conceited and boasted to everyone that she was composing a ballet entitled *The Last Interrogation*. Interrogations at the Alex were unpleasant; mine lasted sometimes from five to seven hours. Always the same questions and the same threats; when I got back to my cell, I would shake from nervous exhaustion. I was unusually lucky that they didn't beat me. None of my cellmates were so fortunate. There were lots of attempted suicides at the Alex—people simply couldn't stand the interrogations.

Sometimes people jumped over the metal railing of the fifth floor landing, killing themselves on the stone floor below.

Mimi and I often talked about suicide. She said that she could not wait patiently like a sheep until they decided to kill us. For a long time we considered this, but finally decided that we must leave to them the moral responsibility for our murder.

Thank God this boring Sunday is finally over; they gave us those same boring books again. That drives me crazy. My sweet neighbour[3] was moved to Section II. I nearly cried. We were the two oldest residents of this wing and I had got so attached to her. For the time being at least, she is in the cell above us and we can talk through the window, only I'll never be able to see her again. Helga, you have no idea how important windows are in prison. If the guards only knew.....

In my mind I can see *Sonnenschein*'s beaming face, a vision that always has such a positive effect on us.

We wish you sunny and happy days during your holiday.

Best wishes from ....your Cloverleaf.

[1]Plotzensee was the prison where they were executed.

[2]Barminstrasse, a processing centre for condemned prisoners from which they went on to Plotzensee, to be guillotined.

[3]unidentified

Dear *Pani* Wanda,

You were once interested in the effect that prison life has had on my disposition and my character. I now have a strange desire to tell you about this, what my thoughts are at this time. Perhaps that is because it seems to me that you will understand this best, and you will see it objectively—not like Mummy who is blinded by her great love for me. I wish to be very sincere. Now that some of your anxiety is eased about Zbyszek, I'm not afraid that I would add to your worries.

Maybe this is completely unnecessary but I would like someone to know more about me, though in the end, it really doesn't matter. It's hard to write this, because it's hard, almost impossible, to find the words to describe all these contradictory thoughts and feelings. Every time I think about Zbyszek, I feel an immense debt of gratitude to fate that he was saved. I doubt that my death will have any long term effect on his life in the future; he is so young. I know now from my own experience how quickly a person can accept and get used to things, which at first seemed impossible to bear.

Thinking about Mummy's despair is far more painful for me than abandoning all my plans for the future, but there's nothing I can do for her. I know that she will never forget this, but I hope that she will not break down, that she will find comfort in religion, in her love for Halinka and her grandson. It will be so hard for her; her love for me is without bounds.

I wouldn't want to exploit the idea that I am a patriot who

died for her country. For one thing, I was initially propelled into the conspiracy by curiosity and a sense of adventure. Only later by love of my country. Still, I do not regret a single step I took, not even now.

However, I did not become a nationalist here, quite the contrary. I consider strong nationalism to be a serious limitation and I always consider myself first a human being and only then a Pole. On the day that I will die, I would prefer to tell myself that I am dying for freedom and justice, rather than that I die just for my own Poland. Consciousness of a universal humanity will comfort me. But please don't misunderstand—it is not that I don't love my country, but I would relinquish my country's objectives if they were not also good for all of Europe and all of humanity.

I am not distressed that I must die. We all know that we must die; the difference is that most people don't know when their hour will come. Death is as natural as life, and that is how one should approach it. If you have a good understanding of life, you know how to accept death. The important thing is to maintain one's human dignity to the end, not to give in at the last moment to an animal-like survival instinct, not to be frightened by that moment of physical pain. But I am sure that we can overcome that, we must summon all our strength for that. We will die free, so free—because prison life taught us to detach ourselves from the minor things that enslave people on the outside. Nobody can imprison our souls unless we ourselves lock them behind the bars of narrow prejudice.

In prison I became—how awful!—much less religious. That is rather odd, but I can't be religious just because there is no other way out. I would think it presumptuous to ask God to save my life, which after all is of no great importance in the universal scheme of things. Why should I have a greater right to life than those millions who have already perished in this terrible war? What will come next, I can't and don't try to imagine. I do believe, though, that the best and the most noble that is in us will not perish, that through this we will unite with something greater than ourselves, that we will approach perfection. It is nice to think that I will meet, in another world, all those I have loved—after all, is it possible that such a powerful feeling as love could just cease to be? Yet to be completely free, one must not love individually but dedicate one's life to the greater common good. But that is for exceptional people, not for me. Because I loved Mimi too much, I now suffer unnecessarily. I can't forget my little Mimi, I can't get over her death even though I have known so many others who were killed.

I have read over my letter and all my conclusions, after so many long months of thinking, struck me as a collection of platitudes. What I had to do, was to arrive at some kind of personal philosophy for my daily use. I had to find a way to achieve this objective: not to lapse into despair, not to lose our spirit even under the most tragic circumstances, and to comfort others. As for death, it is a great comfort to know that when we are gone from this earth, nothing will end or change. The sun will continue to shine, the flowers will blossom, autumn will follow summer, everything will be as it should and always be. What value is one life? Today, it has the least value of anything.

Dear *Pani* Wanda, please believe me that I accept my fate without fear. I am well, and my father's visit gave me great joy. Please kiss all my dear aunts for me, also *Pan* Lucjan[1] and the boys, and I hope that Roza[2], whom I barely know, will get well and return to Warsaw soon. Heartfelt kisses .... Tina

[1]Dr. Lucjan Walc, *Pani* Wanda's husband and Zbyszek's father
[2]Zbyszek's brother's fiancée

Alt-Moabit, Berlin,
29 August 1943

Dearest Mummy,

It's been two weeks since any of us has received a letter
from home. Were it not for Father's visit in the meantime, we
would be very concerned. Perhaps it's only because the censors
are holding the letters longer than usual.

Your parcel, with the box of Camelias, arrived this week.
Thank you. I need laundry powder and toothpaste. Otherwise,
there is absolutely nothing new here, so much so that there's
really nothing to write about. The last interesting thing was
Daddy's visit of over two weeks ago. There are occasional air-
raid alarms at night, but there's been only one big air raid. During
the alarms we have to get up, get dressed, and the doors are
unlocked, closed only with the latch. At night, all the buckets,
cups and bowls we have in our cells are filled with water, so that
we can protect ourselves in case of fire.

Sometimes I have a lot of work, other times less but never
so much that it tires me and I am still in good health. We are
starting to sew heavier dresses though we still make light blouses.
Everything we make is for *Bombenbeschadigte* (relief for bombing
victims). We had really good food this week, that is, once we
got bread with our soup and today, Sunday, apart from the pea
soup we also got a cup of rhubarb compote. In about two weeks
I will see Zbyszek again, because we see him every four weeks
[for cross-interrogation] so I can have the pleasure of looking
forward to that.

And how do you feel, Mummy? You probably worry and

don't sleep at night, and I can't go and comfort you. Alas! Do you realize you will soon see your little grandson? I still think about Mimi all the time and it hurts so much. I must learn to accept something that mere human will can't change.

Kisses from the bottom of my heart my one and only, dearest, Mummy. Give my regards to everyone, especially *Pani* Wanda and Alina.

Your Tina

[smuggled letter]

Dear Helga

Many, many thanks for your loving letters from Gerd [Mimi's brother]; they were so interesting and amusing that we read them several times and we were sorry when we had to hide them again. Last night there was a terrific air raid and so I am quite on edge. I expect that our *Sonnenschein*, healthy and beaming as always, will soon appear. We heard that some of our guards were killed in the bombardment. As we listened to the thundering noise we prayed, "Dear God, don't let the good people get killed." Really, we have never lived through anything like it. The window was open as usual and we could see the blood-red sky and hear the ceaseless roar of the planes and the explosion of the bombs. No, we weren't afraid, just a little nervous, though, for appearances sake we pretended to be calm and even joked. But for one moment we were frightened when we could smell a strong, strange odour and Maria said, "Gas!". Now I know that it was only the smell of phosphorous. I can't believe they would use this terrible weapon in this war; surely that's out of the question. It would be suicide for Europe, since the English and the Americans possess the best known chemicals.

This morning the prison was full of smoke spread here from the raging fires; ashes and cinders continue to float through the air. We are dying of curiosity and can hardly wait for *Sonnenschein* to come with some news. Through the windows people exchange fantastic stories, each more unbelievable than the next. (Hurray! Hurray! I hear *Sonnenschein*). They're saying, for example, that today we won't get any dinner. I had no sooner accepted this terrible blow—with great stoicism—when I heard the sound of the food wagon outside.

And more news this evening—the Americans have landed at Calabria. Complete madness here. I can hardly keep from laughing when I think that we Poles are not permitted any newspapers and I receive two of them: *Lokal-Anzeiger*, delivered from the first floor on a rope, and *Volkischer Beobachter*, which is slipped to me every day when I am out for my walk. Our information services are quite well organized, don't you think?

Ah, that *Sonnenschein* once again brought us a bowl of potato soup; once again I can hardly bend. With my tummy bigger than Buddha's, how can I maintain a very refined posture? My roommates are laughing at me!

We read your letter of Sept. 2. Those shorthand symbols look like nothing more than funny little crawling insects. I can't make it out at all. As for your conversation with the director of a group of girls, I must consider this a little; I have always thought that people who hold such political opinions can't be decent. Before the war—maybe, but now, definitely not. People would have to be completely deaf and blind not to notice such criminality.

Imagine! I just got some heather from a Polish forest in a package from my mother. What an aroma! I was no less happy than you as I buried my nose in those fragrant purple flowers. Marysia's sentence has been confirmed.[1] She'll soon be leaving. The thought of that fills me with sadness which is totally selfish of me. Maria is very precious, clever and prudent. I will miss her terribly.

Well, I must finish now, dear Helga. Keep well. All the best.

Your Tina

[1] Eight years in a concentration camp; the prosecutor had demanded death.

Alt-Moabit, Berlin,
5 September 1943

My dearest Mummy,

After all this time your card dated August 5 and letter dated August 15 finally arrived, along with Halina's card from Trombowla. Our letters must now take some longer route and we can't even dream of mail service like before. Can't thank you enough, dearest Mummy, for the two parcels I got last week. In the first there were toothpowder, shampoo, three apples and candies; in the second the heather which gave me such intense joy, a tin of bacon, and some candy. They let me keep it all because there wasn't so very much. Never send larger quantities than this. I am convinced that your gift ideas are ingenious and in fact you are the best mother under the sun. Therefore I decided to return the favour and send you a self-portrait. How do you like it? I am afraid that for the time being, this is the best you can get.

I can imagine how worried you all are about us as you read about the bombing. We are still a little unsettled by the last one, the night of Sept 3-4. We felt it more because it was targeting this district. We are not afraid though, because we have nothing to lose, but nevertheless, it has quite an impact. The prison grounds were not hit. The next day we were a bit sleepy but then we got better than usual food and so we feel great. You wouldn't believe how well organized the assistance program for bombing victims is.

The heather is beside me and smells of the forest. Do you know how you say heather in German? *Erika*. Pretty, don't you

Christinov Wituske Gef.B.Nr. 1659/42   Berlin - Maalbit, den 5 September 1943

96tlg. I. Zelle 18. Aktenzeichen. R.K.G. III. 16/83

Kochana moja Mamusiu!

Po długiej, długiej przerwie nadeszła wreszcie Twoja Kartka
z 5/8 i list z 15/8, a także Kartka z Trembowli od Halinki. Listy nasze muszą
odbywać teraz daleką drogę, dlatego o tak szybkiej korespondencji jak dawniej nie można
nawet marzyć. Nie wiem jak Ci dziękować Kochana Mamusiu za paczuszki, w ostatnim tygodniu
dostałam dwie, w pierwszej był proszek do zębów, naupomy, 3 jabłuszka i cukierki,
a w drugiej ten wuns, który mi sprawił taką szaloną radość, pudełeczko z boczkiem
i cukierki. Doprawmo mi wszystko, dlatego że było tego niedwio, nigdy nie przysyłaj
mi większych ilości jak teraz Mamusiu, wogóle uważam, że jesteś genialna w swoich
pomysłach i najbardziej Kochaną Mamusią pod słońcem! Wobec tego postanowiłam
się zrewanżować i przysłać Ci mój portret. Jak Ci się podoba? Ten obrazek musi
Ci niestety tymczasem wystarczyć! Wyobrażam sobie, jak się tam wszyscy o nas martwicie,
gdy czytać wiadomości o nalotach.
My jesteśmy jeszcze trochę pod wrażeniem
tego ostatniego, w nocy z 3-4 wrzesień.
Najbardziej go odmieliśmy, bo jego celem
była także nasza dzielnica. Żadna z nas
się nie boi, bo ostatecznie nie mamy nic
do stracenia, ale pewne wrażenie zawsze
wywiera. Teren naszego więzienia zupełnie
nie ucierpiał. Następnego dnia byłyśmy
trochę niewyspane, ale rano dostałyśmy
wyjątkowe dobre pożenie i czujemy się
znów doskonale. Nie wyobrażasz sobie, jak
tutaj wspaniałe zorganizowana jest pomoc

Die Untersuchungsgefangene Christina Wituska —
czyli Twoja Tine.

think? I was so happy to hear that Karol is alive![1] I was so afraid that we would never see him again. Don't you know anything else about him? Where is he? In the East or in the West? Was he taken away for forced labour? This is all very sad for his parents but he'll survive his exile. How I wish I knew what will become of him, what kind of person he will be in future.

And now to answer your questions: black woollen sweaters, blue shoes, and wool stocking were delivered to me at the Alex. I gave the wool sweater to Cezara [Dickstein]. Cezara was my beloved "prison mummy." She came with me from Pawiak [the main prison in Warsaw] to the Alex and for the first two weeks we shared a cell. She was awfully kind and took such care of me. She had nothing warm with her and was freezing, while I had three pairs of warm underwear. Tell Janka Parys's aunt about her—she was her friend at the Red Cross. I gave Zbyszek the woollen socks and the shoes to someone else—they were in any case five sizes too big for me and I looked rather like a Puss 'n Boots. Don't think just because of this that I gave all my things away. I have everything I need but a lot of stuff, in jail, is a heavy load. Besides, I never expected to spend another winter in prison. What a strange coincidence—Aunt Danglowa[2] was for some time in the cell beside me. You know, she is Aunt Krysia's first cousin. I saw her once at the Alex as well. She is awfully nice and all the Polish girls call her "Auntie". Unfortunately she has been sent away to a prison in Charlottenburg.

Please wish Kola a belated, but very sincere happy birthday and thank Halinka for thinking of me. Marysia's sentence has been ratified; it will be sad to part. I should be used to these separations by now, but it's too hard. If only she could have gone to the same camp as Olenka and Wanda. I am trying again to get to see Zbyszek.

Be of good cheer, by dearest Mummy. Your daughter is always

smiling and cheerful.

Kisses with all my heart.

Your Tina

Best regards to Mr. and Mrs. Mierkowski. Kisses to Alina. I got the mirror. Many thanks.

---

[1] No details. Later he disappeared again.

[2] Felicja Danglowa was arrested in the fall of 1942; she was first in Pawiak (Warsaw), then Alt-Moabit (Berlin), and finally in Fordon (Bydgoszcz), one of the largest and harshest prisons for women. Most of the 5,700 women incarcerated there between 1939 and 1945 were Polish.

Berlin,
September 7, 1943

[The letters to Mimi Terwiel's sister and brother were written after Mimi's execution, and were smuggled out by the faithful *Sonnenschein*. Krystyna refers to Mimi here by her formal name, Maria.]

Dear Ursel and Gerd,

I received your letter only on Sept. 6. Thank you for remembering me even during your grief. For that I am very grateful. I had already learned, earlier, that Maria is no longer alive, though I was not able to find out the exact date of her execution. I had no idea that she was killed the very day that she was taken away from here.

I was most pleased by that part of your letter in which you tell me that this misfortune did not break you. I expected as much from Mimi's siblings. Let us hope that she sees all this from above and is very pleased. Nor did Mimi's death weaken me. Quite the contrary. After the first terrible shock of pain passed, I determined that I would follow in my beloved friend's footsteps and bear it as bravely as she. Tears don't help anyone and besides, Mimi no longer needs sympathy; she remains now an inspiration because she died heroically for her ideals. My friends often used to say, "We can't imagine what Krystyna will do when she loses Maria.". But whenever I feel like crying, I remind myself of her words: "Krysia, don't break, don't look unhappy. Don't give them that satisfaction." Then I raise my head and I say, "No, Mimi, I won't break. I will spite them and laugh in their faces." Oh, if only my good, dear parents didn't suffer so! Sometimes, when my situation seems hopeless, I feel so sorry that they didn't let me die with Mimi. Then we would have gone to our deaths with a smile, and we would have shown them how much contempt we have for our judges and our executioners. Unfortunately, like Maria and Helmut, every one of us must take the last, terrible steps alone, abandoned. We die comforted, however, by the certainty that victory will be ours, that we didn't fight in vain for freedom.

Maria used to greet every bit of political news with great interest. Nothing delighted me more than to have some news to share with her. Right up to the end she would spin with me all kinds of fantastic plans for the future, and she avidly studied English. I marvelled at her indescribable enthusiasm.

I want to tell you at least some of the things I know about Maria's life in prison; I think I could talk about her for hours and if I ever get out of jail, I will. I promised her that, the last time I saw her. But since I don't entertain great hopes that this will happen, and each day I fear that they will come for me, I am enclosing these cards I got from Maria. If I live, I will want them back, but in the meantime I want you to have them for safe-keeping. There's one request I want to make: how I'd love to have a larger photograph of Maria; I have just one little snapshot. It's one that Helmut used to carry with him and after his death Maria gave it to me. If my appeal is turned down, I will send both photos back to you. Please grant me this favour.

Three weeks ago my father came to visit me. I gave him your address and asked him to go right away and visit you and give you my warmest personal greetings. I haven't heard yet whether he did. This letter does not go through the censors, but when you write to me, tell me only that you were pleased to get greetings from Maria....[fragment missing]

These are the only letters of Maria's which are still in my possession. We used to write to one another every evening and exchange the cards during our evening walk. I had more than a hundred of them but unfortunately I destroyed most of them for fear of their discovery during a search. The remaining ones are in dreadful condition. For a long time they were wedged in the window, then I concealed them in the hem of my dress. Just now I removed them from a crack in the door. It's lucky they didn't transfer me or I would have lost them all. They contain my dearest memories of her.

I am not given to crying, but when I read the letters she wrote after Helmut's death, my eyes fill with tears. I am filled with rage that she had to endure this horrible pain before she herself was executed. For security's sake, in her letters Mimi called me "Katya" or "Helenka," and she was always my dear "Roxanne." On the day before she was murdered, I got permission to visit her in her cell. I was escorted by a guard who had mercifully granted my plea. Mimi had told me through the window—she was three cells away—that she was being taken to Barminstrasse the next day. We know now what that means, going to Barnim. It's the next-to-last stop, from which the only exit is to Plotzensee. I don't think either one of us ever entertained any idle hopes…[fragment missing]

When we were still at the Alex, Maria learned our national anthem which she often whistled just to cheer me up. She would summon me to the window with the first notes of this song. That evening, she whistled this melody for me for the last time—I have never heard a more beautiful rendition. With the closing bars, I broke down, sobbing in despair. That evening I wrote her my farewell letter and had hopes that I would see her one last time the next morning. The guard had promised me that, but unfortunately she couldn't keep her word. At eight o'clock, I could hear her being taken out from her cell. They took away my most beloved child—Mimi! I didn't realize how quickly she would be taken to Plotzensee. For the next few days I tried desperately to find out whether she was still alive. For a long time they wouldn't answer my questions; finally after ten days I was given the sad news. Though it was so painful, I was pleased that everything ended quickly, that they didn't prolong her torment. Who knows how long her nerves could have stood this terrible strain…[fragment missing]

Alt-Moabit, Berlin
[early September 1943]

[smuggled letter]

Dear Helga.

I am sure there have never been such indulged prisoners at Moabit as we are now. Life is truly splendid for us. Yesterday your Mummy ordered so much pea soup for us that all of us ended up with Buddha bellies and we simply could not move. "Long live *Sonnenschein!*"

We heard today that you were bitten by an ungrateful patient.[1] Does it still hurt?

If I manage to stay alive, I will have to go to see the planetarium. Such things really interest me.

It seems that [the hated prison guard Bauer] "Acetate Slime" might leave us. You can imagine how upset we are about such a loss. We have only one wish—that *Sonnenschein* should be assigned to our section.

I'd better stop writing now or Mrs. B[auer] will tell me, once again, that I consider my work to be of secondary importance.

Thanks so much for the candies; we have never had anything so good in jail before but do keep some for yourself, Helga. All the best,

Your *Kleeblatt*

[1]Helga was working in an animal hospital.

Alt-Moabit, Berlin,
18 September 1943

[This letter was given to *Sonnenschein* to keep and then forward it to the Wituska family after Krystyna's death. Mrs. Grimpe did this after the war.]

Dearest parents,

You will receive this letter after my death. It will be sent to you by a person to whom we are immeasurably indebted. She has been our friend, and our guardian. At great personal risk, she tried as much as possible to ease our difficult fate; she shared with us whatever she could, never asking for anything in return. We called her our "Ray of Sunshine," because whenever she came into our cell, she brought with her joy and laughter. We became friends with her daughter. You saw her once, Daddy; do you remember?

I only regret that I will never be able to repay her for everything that she did for us, for her dear heart of gold. She was especially fond of me and I loved her as one can only love one who offers a hand when you are truly in need and never thinks of this as charity, but only as something normal. Please don't forget her.

Dearest parents, writing this letter I still don't know what will be the outcome of my application for clemency, but believe me that I am completely ready for death and I don't entertain any false hopes. Our long separation has deepened my feelings for you, and it pains me to leave you in such sorrow. But believe me, I am prepared to go to my death with head held high, without fear. This is my last obligation to you and to my country. Prison was for me a good, often difficult school of life, but there were nevertheless joyful, sunny days. My friendship with Mimi will remain with me, an unforgettable and wonderful memory until the end. She taught me to never lose my humour, to laugh at "them," and to die bravely. We will die on the eve of our victory knowing that we did not resist in vain against injustice and brute force.

Don't despair, beloved parents, be brave dearest Mummy. Remember that I watch over you and grieve over every one of your tears. But when you smile, I smile with you.

May God reward you for the love and care with which you enveloped me. Farewell, dearest parents, farewell Halinka.

Your Tina

Alt-Moabit Prison, Berlin,
19 September 1943

Dearest Mummy,

I received your letter of August 22 today. How could I possibly be angry with you? You are always my sweetest and my dearest. I told Daddy that I didn't want to see you only because I was afraid our meeting would be too hard on us, both on you and on me. After such a long time, you are sort of accustomed to my not being there, but after seeing me, it would be so hard to part again. Your nerves simply couldn't take it. And my heart would break to see your suffering and your tears. But if you get permission, do come, and show me how brave you are.

It's a sad day today. Maria is leaving us in a few hours, going to Fordon. I will miss her very much, and it's such a shame she's not going to the same place as Wanda and Olenka.

Don't be offended that I don't write long letters. But what is there to write about? I simply can't forget about Mimi. But I am not unhappy, Mummy. Marysia will tell you some day that I was always the most cheerful one of us all.

Please thank Alina for thinking of me; she sends me such beautiful cards. They give me so much pleasure. I wanted to write to her but it's hard for me to collect my thoughts so I'm putting it off. Maybe I'll write later, if it's at all possible.

Please send me some stamps; I can't get them here anymore. I probably don't have to ask—no doubt you'll be sending me a box of Camelias and some laundry powder. And if you can send me some shampoo, then send either the one with the "little cameo" or the "oatmeal-hops". The others are not very good for my hair.

Dearest little Mummy, try to keep busy all the time and never stay alone so you won't have time for unhappy thoughts; that will make it easier for you.

Heartfelt kisses, my sweetest Mummy, and give my best to everyone.

Your Tina

I need some underarm pads for my blue woollen dress and a new toothbrush.

Best wishes from Lena, the only friend I have left.

[smuggled letter]

Dear Ursel and Gerd,

Your letters were profoundly moving. You are always expressing gratitude, as though I had done heaven knows what for Maria. It was, after all, something completely natural—I loved her and wanted only the best for her. How wretched, how hopeless, my life in prison would have been without her. From her I learned how to bear life with courage, and how to die. No, she didn't want you to know how desperately unhappy she was after Helmut's death. During the week I would lend her my pen so she could write her letters home. On Sundays she always felt dreadful and would say: "Our families must never know how it is here; that would only add to their anxiety; we must at least spare them that." She was very pleased that during Gerd's visit, she was able to remain calm, to bear up. Seeing you that day, Gerd, brought her such joy.

I can't tell you how pleased I am with the photographs you sent. They are marvellous! Now it is easier for me to imagine Mimi's life as it once was …. in freedom. How wonderful it must have been … surrounded by beauty, love and sunshine. You don't think it's a bit much if I were to keep four photos? I just can't bear to part with them. Today is Sunday so I am placing them all around my cell. I gaze at them constantly. There are two large photographs and two small ones. Mimi holding ears of corn, Mimi and Helmut on a knoll in the forest. When my fate is at last decided, I will definitely return these to you. It can't be much longer; it's five months today since my sentence was passed. Today my cell mate was taken away to a penal camp. We marked our separation with a feast of bread with butter and fruit, that you sent us, dear Gerd.

Your letter, Ursel, expressed such love, that I feel a strong attachment to you. Believe me, just as I mourned for Helmut and agonized over Mimi's pain, I now feel even more desperately your loss of Maria. Apart from Helga, I no longer have anyone anymore, with whom I can share my thoughts. To my parents I write only brief, hope-filled letters. That is one thing I can't bear to think about, how terrible my death will be for them. Dear Ursel, were your worries about Mimi not enough that you are now willing to worry about me? When I write honestly, what I really feel, I'm afraid my letters can not always be cheerful. And because of me you can not free yourself of memories of Maria. It would be better for you to forget at last about these tragic times. No, it is neither possible nor permissable to forget, but nor is it good to think about it too much—it can drive one mad.

I hope that work will help you turn your thoughts to something else. But I, unfortunately, can not break with them. I remain in the same cell where, only a few weeks ago, I could still hear Maria's voice. I knew her voice so well, I could always tell right away whether she was sad or in good humour.

I will probably be executed soon. You mustn't feel sad then, dear Ursel. I think that I will see Maria again then—and that makes me happy.

Can you understand that sometimes death is better and easier to bear than life?

I will remember and I thank you, Ursel, that I can write to you whenever I need something. For the time being, my modest needs are looked after by my parents. One thing though: may I send my things to Halensee in the event they come for me? Because we can't send parcels to the *Generalgouvernement* and I would like my parents to get some of my things.

I am so pleased that they sent you Maria's and Helmut's belongings. Were there some crucifixes and Madonnas among them? Mimi was furious that these lovely objects, of all things, should fall into the hands of the Gestapo.

One more thing, Gerd, when you write to my father, please tell him that everything with me is fine. Our letters take four to five weeks to get there. Can you send me some stationery and stamps? We can't buy them in prison right now. We would also like to have a map of the Russian front, preferably a newspaper clipping though not too big so we can hide it more easily. I thank you in advance. As for the cigarettes, they are fantastic!
I never thought that here in this alien land, and even in prison, I would find so many good friends. I am really very lucky! Sending you my very best wishes......your Krystyna

Dear Ursel, I would also like to have a photo of you and Gerd.

Alt-Moabit, Berlin,
[sometime in September, 1943]

[smuggled letter to Helga]

Despite this being one of the tenets of National Socialism, I do think that women should marry and have children because I believe that way our lives will be fulfilled. But why would you have to leave your profession to marry? It seems to me that one can't be so limited; a woman who has nothing besides home and children and wants to know nothing else is as uninteresting as one who understands nothing of family life.

I was absolutely amazed to read in the *Volkischer Beobachter* today this article: "The trio of traitors fled to Palermo and gave themselves up to the protection of the Allies." Of course they are talking about the King [of Italy], the heir to the throne, and Marshall Badoglio. Ach, how I envy those lucky people. No, I take that back. They are contemptible![1]

[1]Italy had been an ally of Germany until it was invaded by the Allies.

Alt-Moabit, Berlin,
24 September 1943

[A smuggled letter to Helga, but from this point on, for safety's sake, addressed to a boy—"Teddy"]

Dear Teddy,

How's your hand? Are you able to write yet? I just got my first letter from Ursel, just as I had given up hope of its getting through. As affectionate as ever. I almost envy you, that tomorrow you'll be able to meet her.

Teddy, Can you fix my pen? I have endless problems with it. It would be such a shame if I couldn't use it anymore. I got it from a good friend who is probably not alive anymore.[1] I've managed to hang on to it through all my interrogations, trials, and prisons, and it's the one Mimi used to write her final letter. You can imagine how I treasure it. It will be yours, when I'm gone.

Teddy, I'm forwarding to you some letters from my friend and neighbour, Jutta. We spent six months together in this section. She expected a death sentence, but—Praise God!— she got eight years in prison. She was taken to Cottbus last week. She's a 25-year-old woman who has a little daughter. What a splendid companion she was!

I must tell you something. Last night, there was an alarm. *Sonnenschein* was on duty, and she came to us. I stood beside her at the door. She caressed my face, and then I held her hand so tightly. I can't explain how I felt; as though I were with my own mother—a feeling of security as I haven't had for a long time.

For a moment I did not feel like an orphan. Are you angry that I stole your mother for this moment?

Teddy! *Sonnenschein* is here and I am writing these words using the pencil you gave me. How can I thank you enough for your presents, for your long letter, and especially for going to visit Gerd so promptly. I am so sorry that he suffered so much on my account[2] The Dragon [a hated guard] did that on purpose. We will now forget all about that and live as "carefree" as before. Poor Gerd sent me what is almost a farewell letter. I'm sure you'll remember to call him and explain everything, tell him I'm still alive and I was delighted to get the cigarettes. I can't smoke them right now, it's still too early, but oh, how lovely they smell. I think the song is lovely, but I wish I knew the melody. You may keep the photographs as long as you like; I don't need them. I am very worried about the bad news from the eastern front. Do you think it would be possible to hold the Bolsheviks at the Dnieper for long? It would be a vile, dirty trick to kill us now, don't you think? If the Dragon had been "lucky", I would now be shorter by a head! That thought does not spoil my appetite and I am terribly hungry right now. I hope that soon we will have supper, with pears from Gerd! Then I will use those horrible black dresses that I have to sew to make a comfortable spot for myself where I will sit and smoke a cigarette. Now I ask you, who could ask for anything more? Loads of good wishes and a big kiss from ..... your grateful Kryscha.[3]

[1]Karol Szapiro, Krystyna's beloved. She must have received word that he was missing again.

[2]Gerd Terwiel thought that Krystyna had been executed after hearing from the Dragon, a hated guard, that one of two Polish girls was going to Plotzensee for execution.

[3]German spelling.

Alt-Moabit, Berlin,
Sometime in September 1943

[fragment of letter smuggled to Helga]

…What luck that you did this, otherwise I'd have been in a fatal mess. I keep reading your letter, and Gerd's, over and over again, I keep looking at Mimi's photograph, slowly sucking a candy all the while, and I just can't believe that all this is for real. Thank you, Teddy, for describing everything to me in such detail, but oh, how I envy you!!!!! Will I ever be able to look at Mimi's picture again, listen to her records of her favourite songs? Please, please write to me everything to the finest detail so that I can imagine that I was actually there. I am so pleased that you are willing to go see him again. So, I will have another letter ready for Friday. It was really nice of you to remember that little poem.

Do you really think that this won't last much longer??? After supper, I pasted the newspaper to the wall with the headline, "Badoglio's Cowardly Treason," so I could feast my eyes on it.

Dear, good God, don't let me die now—when everything is turning out well. I could weep from sorrow that Mimi did not live long enough to see this. She would be delirious with joy!!! How I hate to have to part with your and Gerd's letters today. Teddy, I am so terribly agitated, I can hardly write. Tell me, how can I thank you? Meanwhile, I am sending you a big, fat kiss and lots and lots of good wishes.

Your Krysia

[fragment of smuggled letter to Helga]

…I often used to write home about Mimi and her brother and sister. You must ask Gerd if they received Mimi's farewell letters. I know she wrote them a week before her death. Surely they wouldn't be so cruel as to censor those. That I wouldn't understand!!! Among Mimi's papers, there was a small photograph that I once gave her. So now the situation is that I don't have any photos here with me; they are in a suitcase in a storage closet. Tomorrow I will try to go upstairs and steal them. I have a feeling I'll succeed because as you know, I am by now quite skilled at this sort of thing. I think your photography plans are fantastic! No doubt you will be as determined in this as in everything else. As for the business of the newspaper, I must humbly confess that I only got daring enough to hang it up once I knew that no one other then *Sonnenschein* would be around.

You know, Teddy, when Mimi and I were at the Alex, we used to spin stories for hours on end about a magic ring that could make us invisible. Then, with the big stick that was used for opening the ventilators, we killed our horrible guards and policemen, rescued Helmut, and then all the political prisoners from all the jails and camps. Our storytelling would practically make us feverish, and Mimi would say, "Wouldn't that be wonderful, Krysia, oh so wonderful!"

Teddy, we agree about your name and know exactly how to use it. I like it. But we still have to decide how we are going to write "Krysia"? Should it be the Polish way, "Krysia", or the way

Mimi wrote it, "Kryscha"? She pronounced it so nicely. Germans can't quite pronounce our "sia". So let's keep on using "Kryscha," in memory of Mimi. Dear little *Bazyliszek*, [a little dragon] I wish you good luck in your work and I must finish now or I doubt I will manage to write today to my poor parents. Love and best wishes,

Your Kryscha

[smuggled]

Dear Teddy,

Well, today I had no luck. That witch never took her eyes off me so I couldn't get at my stuff in the storage closet. But I just had to have it, [Mimi's photograph] so I did something I rarely and reluctantly do—I asked—and on the spot invented a sad story about my fiancé, and how much I would like to send him my photo as a last memento. That woman's heart must be made of stone. She just yelled at me. But Krystyna does not give up so easily! I have already registered a request to talk with the supervisor and I will tell her the same sad tale. I am hoping for favourable results but if not, then I will have to hope for better luck and try again to steal them out of storage.

Yesterday we got letters from home which were in transit for over a month, and I also got one from my fiancé. I must now explain this matter to you. I haven't seen this boy in five years; I went off to Switzerland for a year immediately after our engagement. I returned to Poland just a few weeks before war broke out. I didn't see him because he had already been mobilized. He was taken prisoner. Do you know where we finally met after almost four years separation? Here in Berlin, during an interrogation by the Gestapo. Funny, isn't it? I was caught simply because they found my address in his papers, but in fact, our two cases were not at all related. I have no feelings for him and wouldn't marry him if I survived. But I wouldn't break our engagement now, I wouldn't do this to him at a time like this; besides, there is no need to since I will soon be dead. He is still so young. I feel that I am much more mature; I feel sorry for him that he must spend so many years a captive away from his country. He is, all in all, a brave and very decent boy. But really I'm far from being in love with him.

Your letter arrived and I've read it; the best moment of the day is past. I was struck speechless when I saw the grapes, I am still.....[next page missing]

[smuggled letter]

Dear Gerd,

Oh, happy day—your eagerly awaited letter arrived. I just can't imagine life without mail from Halensee.

Thank you so much for those delicious things; these are not trifles you send us dear Gerd. We know that there are shortages in town, so we appreciate it all the more! I would happily starve and freeze if I thought that would make the war end more quickly. I was amused to hear that you find writing letters difficult. I suspect that these difficulties arise from the fact that you don't know me very well yet. Every word from you is all the dearer as I know from Maria that you are very reserved. Wouldn't it be wonderful if someday I could move from Moabit to Halensee. We used to make such plans with Maria and it is really so nice that you had the same idea. What would I do in that strange, foreign town?

Ah, Gerd, if the right moment comes, you will take me from here, right? Had Maria and I only had a file, we would have cut through the grate and escaped; we were constantly plotting this but we never had an opportunity...[fragment missing]

I often wrote to my mother about Maria. She was to pray for her just as much as she prayed for me, especially since Maria's mother knew nothing about this whole tragedy.

The guard that gave us such a scare last week was just here. She wanted to say "good-bye" since she is leaving permanently.

She even wanted to shake hands—what a strange person! But I forgave her everything, because she did take me to see Mimi that last evening.

Dear Gerd, Ursel offered to send me some lingerie, but is it not too forward of me to ask for such things? Nights are awfully cold here and a warm nightdress or a warm jacket would be most useful.

It's getting dark so I must finish now. My luxurious cigarette hour is approaching and I will continue thinking of you.

All the best from me and from little Lena.

Your Krystyna W.

Alt-Moabit, Berlin,
30 September 1943

[smuggled letter]

Dear Teddy,

Thanks so much for fixing my pen, and for the notepad. Would it be too nervy to ask you for something else? It's been a long time since we got any parcels from home. I need some cotton-wool since I haven't received any sanitary packages from home in a long time. The tablets have helped me a lot on two occasions.

You didn't write me a word about Ursel. We are very pleased that your hands are all better. Was the movie good? One more kiss from your K.

When will you go see Gerd again? I had a nightmare about Mimi today. I had to watch her suffer, and I was not able to help her. I woke up sobbing terribly.

[unsigned]

[smuggled]

Forgive me for writing on such a card. You are going to have a lot of problems with my letters if you really want to preserve them all. Could you mention to Ursel or Gerd that little Lena needs a pad of writing paper, and I some headache tablets. Is it still possible to buy a notebook in Berlin? I must go now and read *V.B.* [the newspaper, *Volkischer Beobachter*] Well, dear Teddy, get well soon. All the best—your Kryscha.

Alt-Moabit, Berlin,
Early October 1943

[smuggled]

Dear Teddy,

The Lice Patrol has organized a lice hunt. The stench is horrible. They are trying to gas us! Section Four is so lucky; *Sonnenschein* is on duty there today. But we have seen her today and read your letter. Lena received a lot of mail from home today. Her sister has spoken to my mother, who lives in a state of deep sorrow, because she also gets no mail from me. Maybe she thinks I am already dead? Listen, Teddy, could you send her an anonymous letter? Just one sentence: "Krystyna is well and getting along fine." That would mean so much to her; you would spare her lots of tears and sleepless nights. You are so dear, Teddy, I have to love you more and more each day. I'm delighted with the beautiful poems. Of course I need some Camelia pads, but cotton-wool would also be appreciated if only it's not too difficult for *Sonnenschein* to smuggle it in. Dinner soon. Wonder what slop we'll get.

With a bellyful of potato soup, I now continue this letter. Isn't it disgusting that they force us to work? At least the people condemned to death could be spared this! Instead of that boring work making buttonholes, I would rather study or read. Our neighbour will receive her sentence today, probably death. I am afraid she might not be strong enough morally to take this bravely. I wish her luck. I feel sorry for them, no matter who they are. I am as pleased as you are that you can travel with the (woman) doctor.[1] Kisses from your K.

[1]Details not known.

[smuggled]

My dear Teddy,

I am sorry that you once again went to bed so late because of me. I must thank you for your letter, for all our presents, and your help. Above all for those stolen American cigarettes. You are right, Teddy, my idea about the parcels wasn't well thought out. I myself didn't have much hope that Gerd would forward the card. But you see, Teddy, it would give me such pleasure if I could at least once pay you back for all that you do for me. We laughed our heads off over Gerd's boxer shorts. Mimi got the same kind of shorts from home when we were at the Alex, and every morning and evening, when she put them on, I would laugh myself sick.

I strongly protest against certain secrets between Lena and Gerd! I know that when Lena asks for something for me, she does so with the best intentions, but I know best what I need, and I don't want to load Gerd down with all these requests.

We are so lucky today because *Sonnenschein* is here. She managed to get us an iron and we had something to do all morning.

Forgive me Teddy, but I can't write about anything else today. I am sick with hate and revenge! Our neighbour did get the death sentence of course, and tomorrow is going to Barnim [strasse]. She is brave and serene, she won't shame us—the political prisoners. Last night I couldn't sleep thinking about all the Nazi war crimes. Innumerable crimes and murders. Teddy, what you have seen here is child's play compared to the atrocities they commit in Poland. Yesterday Betty asked me why Germans hate us so much, and consider us "sub-human." This is all their propaganda because they want to take over our country for themselves by wiping out all Polish leadership. They want to justify their bloody deeds. I don't understand why they brought me here to Berlin and proceeded to play out this comedy with the military court. In Warsaw, they simply take two pistol shots, right on the street, to kill somebody. The Gestapo does not bother with ceremony with the Poles. When they took me from my home at night, I figured I had, at the most, a couple of days to live. I had no idea what they knew about me.

My God, if they knew everything, they would have killed me at once! My poor mother was scared to death when I said good-bye to her. I hugged her for the last time and managed to whisper in her ear, "Be brave, and pray for me." I knew right then that this was my final farewell.

Now I know why I am here. The officers and gentlemen here must have something to do so they won't be sent to the front. What very important and hard work it is to condemn all these young girls to death! You know, it amazes me how right-eously they carry out their propaganda about the mass graves at Katyn.[1] Their own methods, after all, are identical. They can "organize" such things very well; in the space of two, three months they emptied the entire Warsaw Ghetto. There were over 600,000 people there. Men, women, children. Nobody survived. They transported the Jews to two great camps in the east part of the *Generalgouvernement*. There they were put to death in gas chambers. If you go past these camps in a train, you can smell the burning bodies. People close the windows and hold their noses. These are not fairy tales, Teddy, I was there. I saw it,

I lived through it. Starving Jewish children, trying to escape from the ghetto, thrown like kittens into the gutters. People shot in the streets like dogs or deported to Germany as slaves. Whenever I was late coming home, my mother trembled with anxiety that I would never return. All Warsaw mothers tremble so for their children—if they still have them—because Polish youth is being tortured to death, killed in prisons and concentration camps. I told you once, Teddy, that the Polish nation is a peaceful one, but you shouldn't be surprised if they are now sharpening their knives and thinking about revenge.

They hate everything German like the plague, because they don't see any decent Germans, only tyrants, murderers, torturers. And this gang of murderers knows too well that if they are defeated, there will be no forgiving. They will try to kill us all, because they would fear the survivors. I became a person eager for revenge, I consider it essential to avenge humanity, to finally exterminate that vermin. Can you understand this Teddy? I curse with fury the Soviet-German pact. Damn them! There, that eases my anger.

Which of Schiller's poems do you want to send me? I have read many of them and my favourite is "Don Carlos." I also had one of Uhland's books once.

We just got our dinner. *Sonnenschein* gave us lots of pea soup. I tell you, Teddy, a full belly is terrible torture; I must sit very erect and move very slowly. But here, my neighbours don't give me any peace—every five minutes I climb up on my sewing machine. They keep calling: "Kryscha. Kryscha." Only once I really jumped, when I heard, "The army is retreating from Naples". That changed my mood!

Can you imagine, today there was no other guard around besides *Sonnenschein*. That is really wonderful.

Will we spend Christmas here? I doubt it. More to the point, will we still be alive a week from now? I don't want to lose hope... hope... hope.

Well, I took advantage of an occasion to get hold of a newspaper, so I will end this letter now. Anyway, *Sonnenschein* will soon come to pick it up.

Best wishes, hugs and kisses to my dear little Teddy........

Your Kryscha

Many thanks for the eraser. I want to draw something for your *Kleeblattalbum*.[2] I don't know how successful I'll be though, I have absolutely no artistic talent.

You must draw something like this for your *Kleeblattalbum*: a white eagle on a red background and these three words, which mean: God—Honour—Country. That would immediately signify that we are Polish and we were fighting for our country.

[1] Katyn: the site of a mass grave found in the USSR. The Soviets murdered over 15,000 POWs, all these victims were officers of the Polish army who were captured when the Soviets invaded Poland in 1939. Despite Germany's propaganda, the Soviets denied their guilt, accusing the Nazis of the crime. It was not until 1992 that Boris Yeltsin finally officially admitted Soviet guilt and delivered to Poland the documents ordering the executions, bearing Stalin's signature.

[2] The *Kleeblattalbum* (The Cloverleaf Album) was a scrapbook kept by Helga in which she collected Krystyna's, Marysia's and Lena's letters. After the war, she turned it over to Krystyna's family and it is currently in the archives of the Main Commission for the Investigation of Crimes Against the Polish Nation, in Warsaw.

Alt-Moabit, Berlin,
5 October 1943

[smuggled]

Dear Teddy,

I feel strange. Sometimes I ask myself, do I still think and feel like a normal person, or like a madwoman? My thoughts and memories torment me. But how can I keep my mind occupied when I have to sew those cursed buttonholes all day? Ahh, if I could only stop thinking. Oh, how I miss my home. For months I didn't experience this feeling. Everything seemed so remote, as though it were just a dream, but suddenly it is again upon me and it hurts so much. What a weakling I am to be writing to you about this when I know so well that nobody can help me if I can't find strength within myself. We must learn to rely on ourselves. This is all egotism; I think too much about myself. When Mimi was still here, I didn't have time for that and I felt much better. [Fragment missing]

Alt-Moabit, Berlin,
6 October 1943

[smuggled]

My dear Teddy,

I am so ashamed of all my complaining in yesterday's letter, but yesterday was exactly two months since Mimi's death. We've been told that you're sick; we're very concerned and feel very sorry for our poor little Teddy. I can never thank you enough for writing to my mother. You wrote exactly what I wished you would write.

I'm really sorry about this, Teddy, but I must once again criticize your countrymen and defend my own. Believe me, I really see things as they are, and I am not influenced by my own particular situation. I am not that limited in my outlook. Nor will I ever go so far as to hate an entire nation.

Much was exaggerated in the news reports here about the war in Poland. You know what propaganda is all about. It's true that quite a few *Volksdeutschen* [ethnic Germans] were killed in Bydgoszcz. The murderers were ordinary criminals who had been released from prison when the war started. This killing was to avenge the Polish soldiers who were machine-gunned by *Volksdeutsche* civilians. Such bloody events are part of the history of all wars once criminals are let loose. I was living in Wartheland, a region with many German communities and no harm came to them, nor in Lodz, for that matter, where there were very many Germans. Do you know any German whose relatives were killed during "Bloody Sunday" in Bydgoszcz?[1] I doubt it. I certainly

don't. On the other hand, I don't know a single Polish family that hasn't lost a son or a father at German hands. What the Germans are doing to the Jews, and to us, is nothing other than cold-blooded genocide. It is guided by the ruthless politics of National Socialism directed against those who are weaker but who will not submit. Why did they send all the priests from Wartheland to concentration camps and close all the churches? They also closed the schools in Wartheland and deprived all Polish children of an education. All Polish leadership was destroyed, Polish farmers and workers are not permitted to study, but are forced to work mindlessly for their new overlords. In Warsaw, they have liquidated half of all lawyers, university professors, doctors, writers, and other professionals. There is not a single secondary school left open. Anyone who wants to continue her education, must do so underground, but this is costly. Germans are particularly cruel in Warsaw because they know that it is there that they will never extinguish the flame of resistance, that there lies the centre of all underground organizations. There, the fight for freedom continues ceaselessly, day and night.....
[end missing]

[1]A city in Poland, the site of heavy fighting in the early weeks of the war.

Alt-Moabit, Berlin,
7 October 1943

[smuggled letter]

Dear Teddy,

Just a few words to send my regards to my dear Teddy Bear.
I am, at this moment, devouring the most delicious honey-cake
and overflowing with gratitude to *S.s.* [from here on, *Sonnenschein*
is usually abbreviated to *S.s.*]. I even got two cigarettes!!!
Today I also received some mail from home that was mailed
very long ago. I got a letter from my sister; what an unexpected
honour!!! The only thing in the whole world that interests my
sister is her little son. She is blind and deaf to everything else.
Pity you can't read this letter!!! It is an ode in praise of her
child's intelligence (he's a year old) and there's not a single word
of feeling towards me. What an odd woman!
Lena sends many thanks for your letter. Unfortunately, she
doesn't have time right now to reply. I must finish now because
S.s. will soon be here, though I would like to gab a little longer
with you Best wishes and kisses,

Your K.

Alt-Moabit, Berlin,
8 October 1943

[smuggled letter]

Addressed to *An Herrn Teddy-Bar*

Dear Teddy,

I feel I must send you at least a few words. I can't manage anything longer right now; perhaps this evening. They seem to think that I have turned into an electric machine, and each day they demand more work. Did the light help?[1] I got another letter from my mother today. Conditions in Warsaw are getting worse all the time. Bandits cruise the streets in their cars, enter any home that appeals to them and take what they want. The villages are terrorized by bandits. Starvation is as common as in India since the Germans have requisitioned everything for themselves. Bringing food into Warsaw from the countryside is strictly forbidden. *My beloved, old Warsaw—how I would love to see you again!* [This last sentence was written in Polish even though the letter to Helga is in German]

We feel quite well. Lena has been terribly busy all day???? (sic) And I am furious because my newspaper carrier did not show up when I went out for my walk. I finish now, with a big kiss and lots of good wishes.

Your Kryscha

[1]Possibly referring to photography. Helga had recently bought herself a camera.

[smuggled letter]

Dear Teddy,

My stomach still hurts from laughing so hard. Have some consideration for us and don't write so many hilarious things all at once or you'll finish us off. We are delighted that you liked the slippers. Lena knitted a pair, just like yours, for me too.

Thanks so much for the poems. I especially like the serious ones; they suit my mood and so my favourite is *"Die Nachtreise i Auf der Winterreise"*.

I've been toying with a new idea ever since S.s. told me that all the guards are taking shooting lessons. Does that mean that they will soon be carrying guns? If so, I have a great plan ready. When one of them comes here in the evening, we will drag her into the cell, bind her mouth with one of the blouses, wrap her head in some of the woollen dresses, tie her hands tight behind her back, and put her on the floor in the corner covered with our blankets and pallets. We will capture her pistol and her keys, and so armed, will exit our cells. (N.B. We must remember to take a piece of sausage with us because, according to Lena, there are some vicious dogs in the courtyard. We can save a little of the sausage from our Sunday supper.) We shall march out to the exit, Lena will open the doors while I stand guard with pistol ready. The men at the door will be astonished, but they will just have to hold their arms up or else they'll get a bullet in the leg. We'll run to the gate and like gazelles we'll leap over the gate and disappear into the night. No, you'll never be able to understand this!

Lena says we must do a practice run. Great, but on whom? There's *S.s.*, but we can't be brutal with her. Ah, Teddy, when I think these things I have to tell you: It would be so wonderful to enjoy freedom once again. I didn't go for my walk today; I just can't stand the insulting abuse and the horrid faces of those witches.

Ach, you know, if my plan with the guns did not work and I couldn't escape, I could at least kill a few Nazis and finally shoot myself in the head. That would be preferable than to be led like a sheep to my execution. Don't you think so?

Tomorrow I will read, and I will write a longer letter to my mother. I have finished the book about the Volga Germans; it was excellent.

You misunderstood me—I wrote that I am tired by the thoughts whirling in my head and not by being unable to think. It is precisely this incessant thinking about the same things that wears me out. I wish it were possible to somehow suspend all thinking, the way one does when asleep. But all of this is unimportant; the most important—that they would let us live! My "fiancé's" mother wrote me that her son's lawyer informed her my situation is mildly improved.

Best regards,

—Julianna [perhaps alluding to a doll she made]

Your Kryscha

[smuggled letter]

My dear Teddy,

We just finished reading your long letter. What a coincidence, I was also thinking of you on Sunday and I made you a little doll dressed in a Polish folk costume. I went to a lot of trouble, trying to overcome my lethargy. Do you like it? To get the material for it, we made two dresses 5cms shorter. The face and hands are made out of one of my slips. (Don't worry, I have another.) I wouldn't want a home in the forest, it's too cold now—or maybe we could sleep in Uncle Tom's Cabin? That would be fantastic! Especially, of course, in the evening!

Reading your story, before dinner, about the venison and gravy, I got furious, but now I can take it calmly, even if you were to write about a roast goose. S.s. saved us from hunger once again. In fact we still have a full bowl of soup and Lena is trying to figure out how to keep it warm. I suggested that she put the sewing machine light into the bowl, or she could sit on the bowl, but she doesn't listen to me. The cake was fabulous!!!!!!!!

We have been thinking for some time, along with Betty and Tanka from cell #20, about making a film about prison life: "The Battle of the Maidens." A worthwhile project.

"*Die Burgschaft*"—absolutely beautiful. Thank you so much for going to all the trouble of copying such a long piece for me. You know, I read this once, but returning to it is all the more pleasant. I also loved the poem about autumn. I can hardly wait to see what Gerd has found for me.

Our thoughts will be with you this evening, my Teddy. I hope you will have less pain. We were so delighted to see your photos. I always think of you as an adult so I am amazed to see before me a teenager—where do you keep all those serious thoughts?

Tomorrow is Wednesday [the day people are taken to Plotzensee, the place of executions] but surely nothing would happen to us the day before you go to see Gerd.

Yesterday I had such pain in my stomach that I kept holding the sewing machine lamp against me all day. Ever since I've been in prison, I feel awful when I am menstruating. The tablets you sent me help. I must go now because those damn buttonholes are waiting. Hope you feel better soon. Best wishes and kisses,

Your Kryscha

How nice of you to think of Maria. I'm sure she'll hold out. Poland needs such women! I'm sure she's always thinking of us and longs for news.

Alt-Moabit, Berlin,
October 14, 1943

[smuggled letter]

Dear Teddy Bear,

Did you go to the doctor's yesterday? I was thinking of you again. I'm worried about Lena. She's had a bad cold for a week, and she's so unreasonable. But there's nothing I can do. She gets offended if I suggest something and, like a child, says that her cold doesn't disturb anybody.

I'm glad you like the doll. I want to make another one for *S.s.* but I don't have any wool for the hair. Do you have some at home?

Wednesday is over, thank God. I'm so glad you went to Halensee. [Home of Mimi's brother Gerd.] I am reading a terrific book; I'm absolutely captivated by it. It's the first part of *Im Wolga Land*, titled "*Die Vater zogen aus.*" I learned quite a few interesting things. There's a marvellous account of a pilgrimage to Aachen. Now I'm reading about the court of Catherine II in Petersburg.

You know I rather doubt that the war will end this year. It infuriates me that the Germans are such good soldiers. How they do this—that is a mystery to me?! I must give them credit, but I would love to see them retreating!

How awful it will be when the Russians enter Poland. And yet I wish for this, because this curse from the east is the only way out.

Lena has gone for her walk; I stayed in the cell. I can hear the water in the pipes; when I close my eyes I imagine that I am sitting at a river's edge. Ah, if I only knew what plans they have for me. October 19 will be exactly one year since my arrest, and exactly six months since I was sentenced to death. It's enough to drive a person mad. I'm closing now and waiting for *S.s.* Best wishes and a big, fat kiss—my dear, little Teddy.

Your Kryscha

S.s. was just here; she quickly deposited a package for us and disappeared. The honeycake disappeared almost as quickly into our empty stomachs. If it weren't for that marvellous taste still lingering in our mouths, I would think the cake was just a dream. I want to send Ursel's letter through you rather than the official way, the censors would delay it and it wouldn't reach Karlsbrunn until about mid-November. The gentlemen of the R.K.G [*Reichskriegsgericht*—the Reich War Court] don't rush these things. I think I'll send Maria a card tomorrow. The worst that can happen is that it will be returned to me. Enjoyed your letter.

[smuggled letter]

My dear Teddy,

Cigarettes—from you? What a surprise! You are an angel; no, more than that—you are an archangel and I send you lots and lots of kisses and a million thanks. Lena bemoans the fact that she is not a smoker, but I can't make this decision for her; I have been considering whether I should give her my portion of the cake in compensation, but that is not a decision I would make in haste. I am so sorry I missed little Julia Hulajnózka's baptism [Julia: the little rag doll K. made for Helga]. In fact, I could have officiated. I am confident that your child will not bring you any sorrows, only joy.

I must finish, Teddy, because I'm afraid of being caught by that horrible Bauer. She was very polite to me today. "Don't look so sour, Krystyna!" she said. What nerve!!! (Did I spell "*dores Gesicht*" correctly?)

Once again, thanks for everything. Until the next time.........Your Kryscha.

[smuggled letter]

My dear Teddy,

I am delirious with excitement! Isn't that girl's escape the most amazing feat? [Stefania Przybyl, a fellow prisoner] She's been telling us all along that she intends to try this but we never took it seriously. We just saw her on Monday at the garment stockroom and spoke to her quite a bit. She was to be executed on Wednesday. She waited until the last minute because she was afraid her escape might affect her sister's situation. Her sister was in the same cell with her. But the last night that she was still here in Moabit, she told us she would escape. She was so tiny, so slender, that she could squeeze through the grate; she had actually tried it a couple of times. But how did she get down from the third floor? Incredible! She did it during an air raid alarm, then crossed over to the second courtyard where she either mixed in with the people coming out of the air raid shelters, or she waited until five o'clock in the morning when the gate is open. She could observe all the movements from her window. Super girl! You can't imagine how I envy her.

She lives here in Berlin and had obtained the status of *Reichsdeutsch*. [Some Poles of German origin were offered the status of German citizenship] but she remained loyal to Poland and worked in a Polish espionage organization. She was in the same conspiracy as Marta Rachel, who is in a nearby cell. Marta is also condemned to death. No doubt they will soon deal with her sister since they were put together the last few days before Stefania was to be executed. How awful she must have felt that she could not escape with her! But at least one got away from the clutches of those bloodthirsty Nazis. We expect there'll be some new security regulations.

Teddy, isn't it awful that my head is too big? I think the grate on the upper floors is wider. That damned grate! Beneath my window is a wall surrounding a courtyard so I could easily then jump to another yard where civilians live so there's sure to be an exit to a street. I shiver just thinking about it. I hope they don't capture this girl!!!

All the best and lots of kisses dear Teddy.

Your Kryscha

Alt-Moabit, Berlin,
October 7, 1943

[smuggled letter]

Dear Gerd,

Another lucky week has passed. Almost every week someone goes to Plotzensee and every Tuesday I think: well, Wednesday is the day.... . I aver it is better to be prepared for everything rather than be shocked by the unexpected. On Wednesday, when the danger is past, our joy is all the greater because we were expecting ...[1]

I want to express my most heartfelt thanks for the apples and the cigarettes. I am only sorry that I am stealing from your already small store of cigarettes. You are no doubt accustomed to smoking while I, for a long time now, have grown accustomed to doing without.

Lena and I were truly touched that you will send us some of your own underwear. We also think it is very funny. I can just see the shocked expression on the head guard (an old maid) when, during an inspection she pulls it out of my bundle. I will tell her a story about my dear, thoughtful brother; I just hope I will be able to keep a straight face.

The hymn to Mary was very beautiful. Our light is on until eight these days. After supper, we arrange our cell as cosily as possible and then we read and write. These are the best hours of the day, when we are left alone. Nobody bothers us, we don't have to look at their twisted faces or listen to their detestable voices. Heavenly peace!

But I don't want silence! I want out of these four walls, this entrapment is a contradiction of life!

From time to time, just as I think that everything inside me has died, I am once again overtaken by a wild longing.

Please give my best to Ursel, I will write to her as well. And all the best to you today from

Krystyna

---

[1]Wednesdays was the day prisoners were taken to Plotzensee for execution.

[smuggled letter]

Dear Teddy,

We maintain our spirit; we will not be subdued!! They put us in chains now at night!!! Bastards!!!

Tell *S.s.* not to cry so much. We love her so much, her tears.... [unfinished sentence]

Kisses ....Kryscha

October 17, 1943

My dear Teddy, I shall continue. Maybe *S.s.* will come here again today. What I wanted to tell you was that we can't bear to see her crying. We have resigned ourselves to our fate [the chains]; it wasn't easy and I cursed mightily—and that got it out of my system. The first night was terrible; we hardly slept but last night we were so exhausted that we fell asleep quite quickly. The handcuffs are old and heavy; they must be from the 18th century and they're very painful on the wrists. I suppose that in time I will get used to this humiliation. Ach, Teddy, you could die laughing watching me pull Lena's pants down when she has to pee. The worst part is that one of us has to go to sleep quite uncovered since it's impossible to cover oneself. I could use a warm jacket and some warm underwear since I gave away my woollen things.

Now that we have such a distinguished neighbour we don't dare carry on conversations through the windows. [A night supervisor was assigned to the floor after Stefania's escape]

Ah, Teddy, things were pretty grim for a while because we were sure we'd be sent to Barnim[strasse]. It would be awful to part with *S.s.*, with you, Ursel and Gerd and then, a new jail again. Better to go straight to Plotzensee!!! We are glad we can remain here. All our guards behave decently towards us and even Miss Bauer was somehow different when she came to put us in our chains last night.

Everything passes; every night of torment is followed by sunshine—today I got a letter from my beloved mother. And Gerd's letter gave me such pleasure.

So long as *S.s.* is with us, everything is bearable. Best wishes and heartfelt kisses to you, my dear, kind Teddy.

Your Kryscha

Little Lena is so lovable and brave. Yesterday she again fell from the window and hurt herself quite badly. Poor little thing.

[smuggled letter]

Dear Teddy,

As you can imagine, I was so emotional on Friday night, I couldn't sleep. Now I must write to Gerd. I regret now that I destroyed so many of Mimi's letters; but I'm really pleased with my luck in at least saving the rest.

Will *Sonnenschein* be bringing us another letter from you? We sure hope so!!! I'm very embarrassed because I think I forgot to thank you for the delicious chocolates.

Teddy, from now on when we write about political matters, let's play a game of opposites, that is, we'll write the opposite of what we mean. Mimi and I used to do that. For example:

Poor, poor Duce, when I read that those gangsters carted him on a stretcher, shackled in chains and loaded him into a van, I cried so much that the newspaper was drenched with my tears. The last newspaper was so tragic and so interesting that I read it aloud to the girls. It depressed us so much. Once the Americans come up against our armies in Italy, then, when we're bombed, I suppose we'll be have to go—of our own free will—to the cellars for safety.

It's a shame that Maria and Lena are not inclined to be enthusiastic. I wish Mimi were still here. She would be cheering like mad. I get so mad when I think about the dragon [guard Bauer] getting yet another victim. I am tough, skinny and not easily digestible. My neighbour from #17 is less sensible than I am—she tried to outshout *Bazyliszek* [Bauer's nickname]. It was a real circus; even the supervisor came downstairs. The poor thing realized that the enemy had a distinct advantage and was forced to capitulate.

Today was Sunday and we should have gone to chapel, but we didn't. A new edict has been issued—foreigners are forbidden to go to church. If we can't, we can't; God won't abandon us just because of that. The Führer himself expressed the opinion that the Almighty will bestow a military cross and a laurel wreath on those nations that, in the hour of their most trying afflictions and most bitter adversity, will not forget their duty to maintain their national honour. So we can be quite sure of ourselves!

Teddy, you have no idea how much it pleased me to learn that you too are capable of great love and admiration for certain people. You know, one friend is all I need and for that friend I would sacrifice anything, even my life. And everything I would do for this friend would be a pleasure and not an obligation. I must admit that because of this I have suffered a lot. But that doesn't matter; the important thing is that my life is not meaningless and empty like that of people who are only tepid, and never passionate.

Teddy, I have a request: If the war should end, or if there is a revolution, would you and *Sonnenschein* please remember to get me out of prison?! I hope I will still be alive when that happens. You know, I wouldn't want to be transported back to Poland along with everybody else. I want to look around Berlin first. What an optimist! Oh, here's *Sonnenschein* with your letter. Dear Teddy, I am frequently overwhelmed by your feelings about everything that concerns Mimi and me. Don't be afraid that the letter and photographs made me sad—it would be a lie to deny it—because at the same time, I was happy that I could tell Mimi's family about everything. I'm sure that Mimi would be very pleased with us. By all means show the letter to Gerd—that will spare me having to write it again for him. And of course you can give him my father's address (just don't confuse it with my mother's address in Warsaw): Felix Wituski, Poczta Brwinów, Majatek Brwinów, *Generalgouvernement*.[1]

---

[1] *Generalgouvernement*. The word "Poland" was banned from any formal usage.

[smuggled letter]

My dear Teddy,

Thanks so much for your letter. We are stitching handbags now—it's utterly depressing. We rarely get out now for a walk—the five of us who are condemned to death, that is. They have taken away all our things though we managed to hang on to our slacks and stockings. Every evening they take away everything including our clothes. At times, we find it all quite funny. Last night, while they were putting on our chains, we had a visit from our distinguished neighbour [the prison director] who enquired whether we were able to sleep. "Yes, yes," she said, "I'm next door and I too can't sleep." (for fear that one of us might escape, no doubt).

Tanka is so small and sweet. They both speak such funny German; I suspect that soon I too will speak that way since I hear this funny language all the time. I'm so lucky, I got a book of Goethe's poetry from the prison library! They're absolutely beautiful!

Ah, you know Teddy, *Sonnenschein* is so lovable, and all the prisoners are so thoughtful, that we don't feel abandoned and we wear our chains—as you said—with pride!

Dear Teddy Bear, thinking of you and your sweet letters helps us so much. They let me keep Mimi's big photo so I will have her always by my side. When you get a chance, tell Gerd that Lena and I send our best regards. Many thanks for the cigarettes; although I can't smoke them, I nevertheless appreciate your thoughtfulness.

Best wishes and kisses from your poor, exhausted but still smiling *Kleeblatt*.

[smuggled letter]

[First part missing] I was discussing my love for Mimi with Maria.[1] She asked me whether it is worthwhile devoting so much attention to just one person; would it not be more profitable to preserve one's passion for greater things. Perhaps she thinks I am exaggerating, though she didn't say so. But she's wrong. This did not make me abandon my ideals. I experienced both happiness and sorrow, but this does not harm the human heart, this does not impoverish a person.

Sonnenschein did not come yesterday. That's when we realize just how much her visits mean to us. We reflect and feel our misery so much more intensely. In despair I sang a song all day about a little butterfly that had to die because he was deprived of the sun. Don't laugh, Teddy! That is really tragic!

Then I received two letters from my poor mother. She mailed them long ago. It breaks my heart to read her letters. She is so alone and for months has been living with this terrible uncertainty. I know that she spends all her days and nights thinking only of me, and praying for me. Her letters reveal her courage and are full of hope, but despite the words, I can feel her pain.

I can't think about this too much because I am falling apart. Cheers! Another Wednesday has passed; and the news is getting better all the time. I have the same request of you as of Gerd: can you send me some beautiful poetry? That would make me so happy!

I am so tired every night, I don't know why that is. Probably because I have so much work to do and I'm so hungry. I don't even feel like talking through the window anymore. Apart from Betty and Tanka in cell #20, my neighbours aren't very interesting.

Dearest Teddy! *Sonnenschein* was just here! I feel better and can breathe easily again. I've just had a sardine sandwich. Today I can fill up on mouldy bread.

Ah, may Gerd's prediction come true and may I soon change my cell in Moabit for a room at Halensee [Gerd's home].

You've thought out the matter of your letter to Maria quite wisely and well. But, Teddy, is it really necessary to let her know when one of us is killed? She will eventually find out anyway. I still have many, many buttonholes to make so I end this letter with best wishes and kisses.

Your Kryscha

[1]Maria (Marysia) Kacprzyk

Alt-Moabit, Berlin,
Sometime in October

[smuggled letter]

Dear Ursel and Gerd,

Your letters mean so much to me. How can I thank you for your kind words and good wishes. It feels so good to know that here, not far away, I have good friends who think of me. I used to feel abandoned in this alien land. My country is so far away! Dear Gerd, I added to your troubles unnecessarily; I am sorry but at the same time I am glad. Do you know why? From your letter I realize that you are not indifferent to me. Mimi's death left a void in my life and you have filled it. For that I am very grateful. I thought about her all the time after her death, but they were only sad thoughts, desperate and terrible thoughts.

There was a splendid storm on Saturday; the cell was in complete darkness, and little Lena went to sleep. I got up on the sewing machine to get near the window, smoked a terrific cigarette, and thought about Mimi. Then I was overcome by a longing to be with you in Halensee.

Thank you very much for the pears, which were delicious. The pencils are very useful. I often think now about the time I spent together with Mimi at the Alex. What we used to do just to get our hands on a pencil, and once we got one, it became our greatest treasure. Life was so primitive then, as though we were living on an isolated island. A pencil, scissors, a mirror— these were our treasures. We used scissors to cut the bread, to sharpen our pencils—they were really a universal tool....

[fragment missing]

I think I once told you about Mimi's neighbour, Henia Weissenstein...

[end of letter missing]

Alt-Moabit, Berlin,
October 1943

[smuggled letter]

My dear Teddy,

Thank you for your sweet letter. We feel fabulous. We roar with laughter every night now because instead of putting handcuffs on both of us, one of us gets these great, thick gloves which can't be removed. It's more comfortable for sleeping but they are really comical, like a boxer. What a beautiful day it is. We went for a walk after dinner and there was a little sunshine in the courtyard. You know, I have never had a kiss that thrilled me so much as the warm caress of the sun on my face; it's been so long since I've felt that. I forgot all my cares and felt happy. We long for news of the world. The chains and this whole monkey circus is not important, the only thing that matters is the war and survival. Survival!!

[End missing]

Alt-Moabit, Berlin,
Sometime after 24 October 1943

[smuggled letter]

My dear Teddy,

You can no longer expect better paper than this from me. [Letter on a scrap of paper] It's just as well that we at least have this boring work and some books. As they told us: "You should be pleased, children, that you don't have to sit all day in chains." I always thought that forcible restraint was used only on dangerous lunatics, but in a Nazi prison everything is possible.

We spend about a half an hour every evening arguing about what type of handcuffs we'll get for the night. During an alarm there is an inspection every five minutes to check whether we are still in our cell.

Let's hope that the little escapee is in a good hiding place and is having a good laugh at the enraged officers and judges.

It's over a year since I came to Berlin. I regret to this day that I did not jump from the moving train. I would have either died instantly or I'd be free now. Those lazy British and Americans aren't rushing to end this war; they're calmly letting the Russians bleed.

[end missing]

This was the last letter written from Berlin's Alt-Moabit prison. Krystyna was transferred to a prison in Halle/Saale in early December.

We know from Helga Grimpe's correspondence with Maria Kacprzyk, that in order to ensure that there would be no disturbance, Krystyna was told by the prison director that she was pardoned. But Mrs. Grimpe saw Krystyna when she was being taken from her cell and noted that she was manacled. She realized immediately that the director had lied. Mrs. Grimpe recalled their last meeting: "She bid me farewell, squeezed my hand, thanked me for everything and smiled—calmly, thoughtfully, and proudly. That's how I will always remember her."

Halle / Saale,
5 December 1943

Beloved parents,

Thank you so much for the lovely things you sent me. I am so deeply touched by your thoughts of me, but I am also sad because I am forbidden to use these things. We have to wear prison uniforms here, however I'm not cold because the radiators are working. I received mail from you a couple of times, Mummy, the last letter dated November 4, with a pretty photo of Kola. Thank you so much for this, my dear sister. Your little one is really marvellous and has such a sweet smile. I often look at his picture.

The parcels that have arrived so far have been given to me. The underwear was included in my things, but please don't send anything else since I get everything that I need here. The only thing I miss are your loving letters, Father, but knowing that everything is well with you, and that your thoughts are with me, I am not discouraged.

I'm afraid that I won't be able to write such long and tiresome letters to you as I did from Berlin. Dear Mummy, I am always so pleased when you write to me about my friends. I am most worried about what's happened to Lena. If you see Mrs. Kacprzyk, thank her for her lovely letter. Has *Pani* Wanda had any news about Zbyszek?

Christmas is approaching again. The last one was also in jail but I was with my friends and my dear Mimi. This year I guess I will be completely alone; my thoughts, of course, are with you, particularly you, dear Mummy, because you are so alone. I hope that Halinka and her little one are now in Warsaw. Wish everyone a happy Christmas for me, and special wishes for *Pani* Wanda, Alinka and her children.

Once again, thank you for all your letters and parcels, for letting me know you are thinking of me. Don't worry about me; I am strong and in good health.

I end with the hope that you will spend Christmas in peace and kiss you all many times.

Your Krystyna

Many best wishes to Halinka and her family; I would love to play with little Kola someday.

Dear, kind Father,

I only had one wish for Christmas and that was for a letter from you. My Christmas wish came true. It made me so happy that I felt completely contented. I am grateful for your efforts to send me parcels; unfortunately I can't accept them.[1] Thank you for the package of underwear and the Christmas present which were delivered to me. I would, of course, write long and frequent letters to you, if only I could.

Dear parents, is it really true that the officers from *Aleja Szucha* said that?[2] I won't celebrate until I know for sure—I couldn't bear the disappointment. I thought about you a lot during Christmas. Don't be sad, Mummy, even if they return all the packages that you send me. During the holidays, I saw a Christmas tree, a manger, and I ate my fill. I'm sure you want to know what my life here is like. It's not possible to explain everything; in any case I am not alone. I really miss my friends and only now do I realize what a priceless gift it is to be among people of equal education with similar perspectives and similar feelings. But I get a lot of wonderful letters. Unfortunately I am unable to reply to them all—*Pani* Wanda, Janka, Lena, and Olenka. Please, dear Mummy, thank them all for me. I get a lot of letters from you though they do take a long time to get here, anywhere from four to six weeks. Your Christmas letter is still not here. What did you do at Christmas?

I gather from your letters that life in Warsaw is difficult and dangerous. Sometimes I worry so much about you and others in

Warsaw who are so dear to me. I often think about Karol [Szapiro].[3] Where can he be? If he were in Germany, he would find some way of letting his parents know. Dear Mummy, please write to Lena; tell her I got her card, I miss her and *Sonnenschein* terribly, and I'm quite sure that of the two of us, she's more fortunate.

Dearest Father, did you get Gerd Terwiel's address? Berlin, Halensee, Seesenerstrasse 16. I would love to know whether anything terrible happened during the bombing. Unfortunately I can't write to him myself.

Dear Mummy, I need [list of hygienic items]. Print in large letters on the package: "Hygienic supplies;" I think they'll let that through. But please don't send any food; there's no point. I was delighted with Olenka's letter. I am pleased that things are going well for Zbyszek in Berlin, though I doubt that he'll be sent home after he has served his sentence. The Germans need labourers. Ask *Pani* Wanda to give him my best wishes. Dear Mummy, I am so happy that after all this time you can finally sleep a little more easily. I'm sure this waiting is harder on you than on me. I hope that after all these endless worries I've caused you, I will also bring you some joy.

Best wishes and kisses——your Krystyna

Health and happiness to our landlords.

[1] Regulations at Halle-Saale were very severe.

[2] *Aleja Szucha* is the Gestapo interrogation centre in Warsaw, its name taken from the street on which it was located. The Gestapo in Warsaw must have held out some kind of promise to Krystyna's parents, either that they could visit her, or even that she still might get a reprieve.

[3] Maria Kacprzyk recalls that she heard while still in prison that Karol had been arrested and shot. Krystyna's parents must have wanted to spare her this news.

Dearest Mummy,

It was so nice to finally get all those belated holiday greetings. Leszek's poem was so moving; I thank him from the bottom of my heart. If I could, I would write long letters to everyone who wrote to me. Please thank Lena and tell her how pleased I was to get her letter and the photo of Teddy. I received some of your packages. Thank Mrs. Kacprzyk[1] for her affectionate letter. She finds it hard to understand that Marysia misses Moabit, but I feel exactly the same way. Despite the very severe conditions, we felt in a way like girls in a very strict boarding school. Mummy, don't worry, I will not break down psychologically. I am not a weak little girl anymore. If one is not a weakling and does not break down at the start, then misfortune makes this person even stronger and more resistant—and this is what happened to me. I get stronger with every day that I am forced to live far from you. Still, I must admit that sometimes I wish I could once again be a child and in your arms.

Dear Alina, thank you so much for your kind thoughts. The few lines you wrote are as lovely as a poem. My conversations with my cell-mate are not, I'm afraid, at the same level as ours were. Kisses to you and your little ones.

Dear *Pani* Wanda, how can I thank you for your kindness? Reading your letters I am able to lose my feeling of loneliness, if only for a while. I feel as though I am with you and not like a fallen leaf, blown by the wind across the earth. I hope today's letter will reassure you. You see, it's just that I have too much time on my hands and sometimes this shows in my letters, but I am definitely not weakening, not "failing in spirit." If that were so, I would blush before all of you. Today's trials are not so important really; when this is all over, we'll quickly forget these difficult times.

Please thank everyone who signed the letter—and give my best wishes to the young couple! I envy Niki his work in the forests. Tell him how grateful I am for his faithful friendship.

Dear Mummy, I have to tell you something even though it breaks my heart—you are not permitted to write to me so often! Best wishes and kisses to all my loved ones in Poland, and you Mummy, most of all.

Your Tina

---

[1]Marysia's mother

My dear parents,

You must be relieved and pleased now that Mr. Greeve[1] has given you a full report that I am in good health and spirits. I think it was awfully kind of him to go to so much trouble for you, Father. I expect that you immediately told Mummy every word. I can hardly wait for his arrival and simply don't know how to occupy my mind for the next few, long, hours. It is really curious that despite the uncertainty of my situation, I am drawn so strongly to study. By the way, it was very pleasant talking to Mr. Greeve about you, Father, and about your work. You are a splendid person, which of course I have always known, but it was lovely to hear it again.

Thank you, dear Mummy, for the package with the sanitary pads and toothpaste. It would be better if you were to write your letters in German. The last letter I got from you is dated January 28. I want to reassure you again that I am not freezing; I can sit or stand all day in front of the radiators. I'm sure there aren't many people in Warsaw who have such warm rooms. You see, I worry more about you, how things are and will be for you; I'm sure things will get worse in Warsaw. Write me right away and tell me where Niki will be after he is released. I assume he was lucky this time! Sorry, Mummy, but I need another comb. These stupid things probably cost a fortune in Warsaw, but I'm afraid I broke my comb again. I also need some hair clips. My wisdom tooth suddenly decided to act up and caused me a lot of pain, though I did get some tablets for that.

Do you think I don't know what is happening to Lenka? I do know, I know exactly. I don't envy her; I'm only glad that she has good friends and good books. It's been four months since I've heard a single word in Polish. I could improve my German I suppose, if my cell mate spoke a decent German instead of *Plattsdeutsch*. Though I do have hope, I can't allow myself to count on winning because there's no further information. I wait and I am grateful at the end of each day that I am still alive. I think of you and knowing that I have you, I am actually happy from time to time.

Another winter in prison is soon coming to an end, and one doesn't really feel like dying in the spring. I was sentenced to death on a lovely spring day [April 19, 1943], the kind of day that makes one want to shout with joy, "I'm alive!"

Give my best to all my friends, to dear *Pani* Wanda, to all the good aunts and everyone who thinks of me. Special regards to faithful, old Miss Tola. Don't worry about me, dear parents. I am well and strong.

Love and kisses,

Your Tina

[1] Mr. Greeve is a German acquaintance of Krystyna's father's who visited her in prison.

Mummy,

You are the best and the most loved Mummy. Every letter and package from you reminds me of this. I know that many people are thinking of me, but you, it's as though you are always with me. Don't you agree? I could lose faith in everything in the world, except your love for me. The comb and the sanitary pads arrived; nothing is missing. I love the sweet smelling soap and the colourful card. Set on my little table during Easter, it cheered up this monotonous cell. You can't imagine how much I liked looking at the little yellow chicks. And at the sight of the little Pascal Lamb I cried thinking how much you love me and I can't even kiss you. Oh, Mummy, sometimes it's not so easy to be brave, especially at moments when I am overcome with homesickness. I'm sure you feel the same way. But we shall overcome this—right, dear, brave Mummy? I received your letters of March 20 and April 9. For two weeks, including the holidays, I was alone. Now I have company again. I'm almost finished my Italian book—it's amazing how much I learned in such a short time. I can see the top of a chestnut tree outside my window; what a pleasure to watch the leaves grow and the flowers bud. The sun peeks in after dinner. April 19 marked a year since my death sentence; my friends are probably thinking of me as I am of them. When do you expect Wanek to visit? Where is he now? Thank you Janek, for your loving letters. I kiss you dearest Mummy, and you Halinka, Janek and little Kola. Best wishes to Mr. and Mrs. Mierkowski, Leszek and Janusz.

Beloved, wonderful Father. I received your letter of April 2

Krystyna, her sister Halina and their mother.

and I was so pleased to read your words of praise for my endurance. Admiration from you is doubly pleasing because I know that your standards of behaviour are very high. You see, I never forget that I have courageous parents; how I wish that someday I could bring you happiness. You know, there was a time when I wanted everything, but not anymore. I don't miss anyone but you and Mother. I have lived through enough and I learned a lot about human nature. Now I want only you, my parents, and to walk together with you over the broad meadows at home. And I am fully aware that nobody in the world can help me now and I must deal with my sorrows myself.

Dear *Pani* Wanda. Mummy told me such sad news and I can imagine the sorrow in your face. If only I could comfort you. I desperately want to believe that *Pan* Lucjan [Walc] survived his illness; and perhaps you've had news from Zbyszek by now. It was inevitable that after he served his sentence he would be transferred to *Staatspolizei*, and if he is in the *Polizeiprasidium*, he will only be able to write after four weeks. He might be sent for forced labour which is infinitely better than to be sent to a camp. If you happen to have a chance, please forward the following words to him.

My dear friend, I fear you may remain behind prison walls for a while yet, though I would be so happy to hear that you had better luck. My dear, good, faithful friend, thinking of you helps me through many difficult hours. It is foolish to be thinking about the future while I remain on the abyss. You know yourself how often in moments of despair one must hold on to something strong as a rock just to survive. My rock was your love. Thank you, dear Zbyszek. I worry about you sometimes, but I want to believe that everything will turn out fine. Stay well. All my best,

Your Krystyna

Halle / Saale,
13 May 1944

My beloved parents,

My birthday was wonderful. I experienced so many pleasures all at once that I am once again radiant and happy as I haven't been in a long, long time. I write this letter full of hope because I want to believe that the most difficult times are behind me and that before long I will be able to inform you about the final decision concerning my fate.

For some time now I've had more freedom, I've been moved to another cell and I am permitted to wear my own clothes. On my birthday, everyone here was very kind and warm, and I got my mail—a letter from Father dated May 4, a notebook, a postcard and a parcel. Thank you so much for the birthday greetings and for everything else. You can imagine, Mummy, how delicious everything was! Your letter of April 27 and the comb were delivered earlier. Now I have two combs and I'm sure I won't break them again. My hair was really falling out so I cut it very short. Some people flatter me and say I look like a school-girl, but I'm sure they think I'm a plucked chicken. Please be so kind, Mummy, as to ask Dr Walc [*Pani* Wanda was a dermatologist] if she has anything that might strengthen my hair, and send it to me.

My only care now is for Zbyszek. It's almost certain that he's stuck in another camp. We just have to be patient until he gets a chance to write since 'stapo [the Gestapo] doesn't send any news. I've been hoping for a letter from *Pani* Wanda but I guess she's too busy, what with Uncle Lucjan being so ill.

For the time being, I am alone in my cell, just me and my books, but I'm not bored—quite the contrary; I'm resting and enjoying the tranquility. I've finished the Italian book, so now I'm going over Italian grammar which gave me a little trouble. I began writing exercises from the start. Thank you for the news about Lena. It's wonderful that Janek can go to the country again with his family but I'm sure you will miss your little grandson terribly. Right, Mummy? After all, you must have someone to look after and to spoil!

Ah, Father, how splendid it would be if you could come and visit. Bring your permit from the military court like you did last year; since the death sentence is still hanging over me, you'd better hurry because we don't know how long I'll be here—maybe it would work!

Thank you for your letter, dear Janek. I would have gladly responded to your philosophical observations about happiness if only I had a bigger piece of paper. One thing is certain: Happiness as a permanent state is impossible, but even a prisoner condemned to death can experience moments of happiness. As you put it so well, it is, after all, a spiritual matter. There's a beautiful chestnut tree in full bloom outside my window. If you hear a chorus of nightingales singing in Brwinów Park some evening, please think of me. (The chestnut in bloom seems to have put me in a romantic mood.)

Keep your chin up, Mummy! I am well and always thinking of you. Give my best to *Pani* Wanda and Mrs. Mierkowski. Kisses to you, Halinka and little Kola.

Your Tina

Dear Parents,

By now you must have received my letter in which I described my wonderful birthday. Things continue well. If I worry at all now, it is about you; as for myself, I believe that since luck held out for me even in the most dangerous times, so it will continue. I can imagine how you tremble when you hear about the air raids in Germany. Stay calm; during an alarm we all go down to the cellar. I was delighted to get your letter and Janek's card of May 10, as well as a letter from *Pani* Wanda. I am now certain that Lena's sentence was commuted and she was sent to a penal camp. Ach, Mummy, I had thought that prison had smartened me up, but unfortunately I've decided that I'm a long way from smart. But then, such a conviction must also be a sign of some intelligence.

What are the chances of a visit, dear Father? To be quite honest, I don't think this journey is possible right now. I have a great favour to ask. Please send, or bring with you: laundry powder, a small mirror, a washable summer blouse, and some blue, dark blue clogs. My writing was improving. What a shame my studies had to stop.

Dear Janek, thank you for your letters and your heartfelt interest in me. I hope that Halinka and the little one feel well in their home.

You were asking, Mummy, about my companions, but it is hard to answer that. In the last little while, I frequently changed cells; for the time being I am alone, but I won't be here for long. Give my best to my friends and to all who think of me.

Heartfelt kisses to all,

Your Tina

Halle / Saale,
18 June 1944

My dear parents,

Mr. Greeve's visit was a great pleasure for me. By the time you get this letter, you will have heard about me, about my good spirits, that my work is light, I am not alone, and I manage to hold my head high.

Dear Mummy, Mr. Greeve said that they think Warsaw might be bombed, and I'm quite worried about you. Let's hope our home will be saved.

I received everything that Mr. Greeve brought here. You can imagine how happy I was. I don't know whom I should thank for these lovely and useful things. The shoes with a cork sole fit like a glove and are beautiful. I wore them all day today and had no desire to take them off in the evening; I could sleep in them. The blouse is exactly what I wanted, pretty and practical. The boots are not very useful at the moment. The soap and other toiletries are, as always, much needed.

Dear, sweet Father, it would be so wonderful if you could come! Mr. Greeve once again held out hope. I think that unlike last year, this time there would be no need for us to keep up appearances while deep inside we querulously wonder: "Will we ever see one another again?" I also received your parcel for Pentecost, and also a package of toiletries including the hairbrush which I really needed. You are an angel and you think of everything. This is not the best paper in the world, but I hope that you'll be able to make out my writing. Day before yesterday there were two letters (an especially happy day!) one from Janek dated June 5 and one from Mrs. Kacprzyk. Please thank her.

I'm glad that our dear Maria is in good health and spirits. At present my life is not as lonely as it was during the winter months; since I meet many women at work I don't have much time to dwell on my problems. The days pass quickly, and every evening I feel happiness, thinking that soon I'll be free.

You ask about my companions. Until recently there was nothing interesting about them but a couple of weeks ago I found a friend who is very sweet, good and clever, and we got along very well. Unfortunately we couldn't stay together. I'm sure you understand that this is very hard on me. You know what I'm like; when I find someone who is interesting, my friendship knows no bounds. I'm still like that so it is depressing to be alone while not far away there's a person from whom I could learn something. It would be best if we could stop feeling anything while in jail—or so I sometimes think—but in fact after you have shed your tears because a friend was killed or taken away, the happiest memories are those of loving friendships. Tears dry, worries are forgotten, but the memory of a beautiful friendship will shine even during our darkest hours. The image of Mimi never fades, and has supported me through many a dark, winter day. The thought of death is made lighter knowing that she has already taken that road. But don't think that these tragic events have made me melancholy. Quite the contrary, I have learned to find joy in life, to think of every beautiful hour as a gift from heaven. Poor Jurek! What a pity to lose such a marvellous youth. And I can't really believe that Karol is no longer alive!

Dear Father, if you can come, please bring me the suitcase, which I will need if I am sent away in a transport. Once again, many, many thanks and best wishes.

Your Krystyna

Halle / Saale,
26 June 44

Beloved parents,

How hard it is to write this last letter. But you must believe me—I am not afraid of death, I do not regret my life. I only think how much sorrow I give you, how you will grieve during the last hours of my life. I want to thank you again for your care and your love, for your unconditional dedication, my dearest Mummy! I can never thank you enough for everything you have done for me, for my joyful, carefree childhood. Don't cry, Mummy, may God ease your pain. I know that you long ago forgave me all the trouble and worry I caused you. I am looking for words that would help me cheer you but I can only think of one sentence that *Pani* Wanda said when she lost Lolek: "God's best-loved die young."

I am completely at peace, believe me, and I will remain serene to the end. My last obligation to Poland and to you—is to die bravely.

Beloved Daddy, dearest Mummy, I feel you are with me today and I am so conscious of my great love for you. I dedicate my last thoughts to you. Be brave! Bid me farewell.

Your Tina.

[On the other side of the page was a German poem]

Viel des Edlen hat die Zeit zertrummert,
Viel des Schonen starb den fruhen Tod,
Durch die weichen Blatterkrame schimmert
Seinen Abschied mir das Morgenrot.
Doch um das Verhangnis unbekummert
Hat vergebans euch die Zeit bedroht
Und es rauscht mir aus der Zweige Wehen:
Alles Grosse muss den Tod bestehen.

Much that was noble, time has destroyed
Much that was beautiful, death has cut short
Through the soft canopy of leaves I see
The fading shimmer that is dawn's farewell.

Yet heedless you approach your doom
And time threatens you in vain
For the sighing branches whisper to me
All great things must die, to last.

Spokesman of the Military Court

Torgau, 10 July 1944
Zietenkaserne
Telefon 933

Mr. Felix Wituski
Majatek Brwinów pod Warszawa

Your daughter Krystyna Wituska was sentenced by Military Court 1. Senate – on April 19, 1943 and condemned to death for spying, consorting with the enemy, and betraying the State.

The sentence was confirmed on May 21, 1943 and carried out on June 26, 1944 at the Halle-Saale prison following refusal of clemency by the Führer.

Your daughter's last letters are enclosed.

Prepared by:
[signature illegible]

Inspector of Military Court

Dr. Fleischmann (signed)

[Letter to Mrs. Wituska written by Helga Grimpe on behalf of her mother Hedwig. Krystyna's mother had written to Mrs. Grimpe thanking her for the care and affection she had given her daughter while she was at Al-Moabit Prison]

Berlin,
12 Dec. 46

Honourable lady,

I can only assure you without exaggeration what happiness I felt reading your first words to me. You lifted from me a very heavy burden. How often I wanted to write to you! But every letter ended the same way: in the fire, torn up, destroyed because of the awful conviction that in your eyes they may seem to be lies and hypocrisy in view of the fact that it was Germans who tormented Krystyna and pursued her to her death. I am German and so I can't help but feel responsible for all the deeds and atrocities committed by my nation. Therefore Krysia's death, as all the others, will always be, for me, a terrible guilt. Please don't thank me! For what? What could I do for Tina—or, in fact, what did I do for Tina?

I have much more to be grateful for to Krystyna than she to me. Her courage, and that of her friends, proved to me that I must honour the Polish nation, all Polish people.

I feel an obligation to go to Halle-Saale, to see if I can get more information about Tina. As soon as I get permission and documents to enable me to take the trip, I will go there and of course I will not fail to inform you of everything that I can.

I want to assure you, that I will do anything to earn your

respect, and if possible, your friendship. I will try to do everything possible so that you will be able to believe that there are better Germans.

In this spirit, I send you my best wishes and remain ever in your service,

Helga Grimpe

Family and Friends
An Annotated List

RITA ARNOULD
Executed August 19, 1943 at Plotzensee.

CEZARA DICKSTEIN
Transported to Alexanderplatz with Krystyna, sent to Ravensbruck.

HELENA (LENA, LENKA) DOBRZYCKA
Arrested in mass arrest (43 persons) of underground members in Gdansk (Danzig). Condemned to death in Berlin, but sentence commuted. Sent to Stutthof concentration camp in February 1944, and escaped from forced march during evacuation of the camp in March 1945. Of the 43 arrested, 39 were executed, one was sent to Auschwitz where he died, one survived Fordon prison, and one is unaccounted for.

MONIKA DYMSKA
Guillotined June 25, 1943, aged 25, in Plotzensee prison, Berlin. Her father was killed at the Oranienburg concentration camp, mother survived Ravensbruck concentration camp for women, sister, Irena, and brother, Meczyslaw, survived imprisonment and torture at Fort VII in Torun.

JANEK
Identified only by first name, an escapee from Auschwitz, removed from Alt-Moabit and never heard from again.

CHRISTINA JANEVA, "TANKA."
The Bulgarian prisoner in the cell beside Krystyna. She was executed at Plotzensee.

OLGA (OLENKA) JEDRKIEWICZ
Transported to Alexanderplatz with Krystyna and cell-mate at Alt-Moabit. Sent to penal camp, Witten-Annen.

WIESLAWA JEZIERSKA
Age 31, guillotined at Plotzensee March 9, 1943, with her colleague Olga Kaminska.

Maria Kacprzyk

Arrested with Krystyna, transferred from Pawiak prison in Warsaw to Alexanderplatz, then Alt-Moabit in Berlin. Sentenced there to eight years in Fordon Prison.

Olga Kaminska

Sentenced after giving birth to a son who was taken to a German orphanage. She was executed at Plotzensee on March 9, 1943, aged 21. Worked as courier/escort for escaped POWs across Yugoslav border. The seven women who were couriers were executed.

Wanda Kaminska

Arrested with Krystyna, transferred from Pawiak prison to Alexanderplatz, then Alt-Moabit, Berlin. Sentenced to three years in penal camp Witten-Annen.

Stefania Przybyl

Escaped, sister Helena Mackowiak guillotined at Plotzensee Oct. 17, 1943, aged 36; mother and another sister subsequently arrested.

Marta Rachel

Friend of Stefania Przybyl's, executed.

Karol Szapiro

Arrested at a railway station and shot, details not known. Fate of parents unknown.

Maria (Mimi) Terwiel and Hans Helmut Himpel

Guillotined at Plotzensee, Berlin.

Zbyszek Walc

Prisoner-of-war Oct. 25, 1939 in Stalag II Neubrandenburg. Turned over for forced labour in March 1942. Arrested by Gestapo in fall 1942, trial at Alexanderplatz Prison, then Alt-Moabit Prison. Sent to concentration camps, first Sachsenhausen then Buchenwald. Burned to death in barn along with other prisoners during forced march in last weeks of the war.

Wanda Wegierska

Arrested April 1942, tortured in prisons in Lodz, Warsaw (Aleja

Szucha) and in Aleksanderplatz, Berlin. Guillotined April 25, 1943 aged 24. Father, Edward, arrested Oct. 13, 1939 in Lodz, deported to Sachsenhausen-Oranienburg where he died in May 1940. Mother imprisoned in Lodz; brother killed in Auschwitz Aug. 12, 1942, sister and sister-in-law survived Auschwitz.

Alina, Krystyna's aunt and children survived, although her husband was killed in battle. Krystyna's parents, her sister Halina, her husband Janusz, and their child, "Kola," also survived.

OTHER TITLES OF INTEREST FROM VÉHICULE PRESS

Maurice Podbrey
Half Man, Half Beast: Making a Life in Canadian Theatre

Timothy Lloyd Thomas
A City with a Difference: The Rise and Fall of the Montreal Citizen's Movement

Philippe-Joseph Aubert de Gaspé (translated by Jane Brierley)
Canadians of Old: A Romance

Fraidie Martz
Open Your Hearts: The Story of the Jewish War Orphans in Canada

Raymond Beauchemin and Denise Roig, editors
Future Tense: New English Fiction from Quebec

Ann Charney
Defiance in Their Eyes: True Stories from the Margins

Matthew Friedman
Fuzzy Logic: Dispatches from the Information Revolution

Jacques Poulin (translated by Sheila Fischman)
Mr. Blue

Sherry Simon, editor
Culture in Transit: Translating the Literature of Quebec

http://www.cam.org/~vpress